BUDDHAHOOD

BUDDHAHOOD

Phiroz Mehta

Edited and introduced by
John Snelling

ELEMENT BOOKS

This edition first published in 1988 by
Element Books Limited
Longmead, Shaftesbury, Dorset

Printed and bound in Great Britain

Designed by Clarke Williams

Cover design by Ariane Dixon

Cover photo: Jimmy Holmes/Himalayan Images

British Library Cataloguing in Publication Data
Mehta, Phiroz, *1902-*
Buddhahood
1. Buddhism
I. Title II. Snelling, John, *1943-*
III. The Middle Way
294.3

ISBN 1-85230-055-8

Dedicated to

G F
B L Jenks
Rosemary Monk
John Snelling
with sincere thanks and esteem.
P D M

CONTENTS

ACKNOWLEDGEMENTS

It was originally planned to publish the present volume privately and a notice inviting financial support was accordingly inserted in *The Middle Way*. Fortunately, our financial problems were summarily and completely solved by the kind intervention of an unknown benefactor associated with our publishers, Element Books. We would, however, like to thank sincerely all those who promised support, even though in the event their kind offers did not have to be taken up; they include Maria Andreanszky, Peter J. Burrell, Joan Fuller, Pat Griffiths, Ann Hawkins, Eva Hookway, Michael Leigh, Rosemary Monk, John and Maxine Saban, Ian Shipman, John and Sylvia Swain, Dr Noel Thomas, Pat Thurston and Philip Warren.

•

Gratitude must also be recorded for the good work of those who transcribed some of the items republished here. Unfortunately, many of the willing hands who did this work cannot now be traced, but we can pinpoint Judith Clarke (who transcribed 'The Nature of Meditation' from tape) and Anne-Marie Warmington (who transcribed the lengthy taped interviews published under the title, 'Living the Good Life').

EDITOR'S INTRODUCTION

We live in strange times. In the West, our religious traditions dessicated from having been long cut off from the well-springs of direct mystical experience, we reach out desperately for anything that will slake the pangs of our vast spiritual thirst. Significantly, we have turned to the East for its wisdom—but, in our haste and despair, have taken on board much that is spurious or debased. Recently, the dramatic rise—and inevitable fall of a number of super-gurus, all equipped with powerful publicity machines and spawning mass cult followings, have naturally attracted much media attention. Effectively marketed, a super-guru can, it seems, achieve fabulous wealth and fame (or notoriety). He dispenses a few superficial teachings and practices, assuring the gullible that the ultimate spiritual blessings can be secured quickly, with little effort and often without relinquishing any of the venal satisfactions of modern consumer life.

•

How far all this is from what the situation must have been like in India 2,000 and more years ago. No easy routes to the spiritual heights were offered then. The great *shramana* (ascetic) teachers, who must always have been in short supply because of the extreme rarity of the qualifying factor, Enlightenment itself, tended to shun the centres of population and the haunts of commerce, preferring instead the comfortless seclusion of forest and mountain retreat. Few disciples gravitated to them, simply because there were no illusions as to what the great teachers expected of those aspiring to live the *brahmacarīya*, the holy life: not money or slavish adulation, but simply the readiness to cast aside everything—literally *everything* that was not conducive. This invariably meant submitting to rigorous asceticism, though there were inevitably differences of degree.

•

But even in a spiritual dark age like our own, the light is never completely extinguished. It survives, transmitted by a handful of true luminaries, who shine all the more brightly amidst the prevailing gloom. The late Jiddu Krishnamurti was one; the author of the essays collected in this volume, Phiroz Mehta, is another. Both can be fairly called authentic sons of the great Indian spiritual tradition.

Anyone who makes the unlikely pilgrimage through the desolate urban sprawl of South London to Phiroz Mehta's home in suburban Forest Hill, will come away with a sense of having spent time in the company of a great spirit: *a mahā ātma* or *mahātma*, as the Indians would say. It is not just a matter of hearing deep wisdom enunciated in well-polished words and receiving good counsel; the profound silences between the words play their part too, and one is mysteriously touched by a gentle harmonizing power that dissolves all inner discords and, for the moment at least, restores the heart to its native tranquillity.

•

Phiroz Mehta has lived the modest life of an ordinary householder, marrying and raising a family, to support whom he worked firstly as a lecturer on Indian religion and culture and later, down to his retirement, as a schoolteacher specializing in science. He has written four major books and numerous articles, been a tireless and inspiring lecturer, organized summer schools and held regular group meetings at his home for many years. Yet he has never sought to elevate himself as a master or guru but has remained always the humble 'fellow student', proclaiming like Socrates that his vast learning has merely shown him the enormity of his own ignorance. He has been—and still is—ever ready to be of service with information, advice and encouragement to all-comers. This life has not been an easy one; the physical cost of bearing so many burdens has been great; but it has been joyfully borne—not only by Phiroz himself, but also by his loyal wife.

•

In more ways than one Phiroz Mehta has contrived a happy marriage of East and West. Born in India in 1902 of Parsi parentage, he was brought up in Sri Lanka, educated at Cambridge and has spent the greater part of his life living and working in Britain. In 1939 he married Silvia, the daughter of Dr J. H. Shaxby; two fine sons were born of the union. But in a deeper sense, his life's work has been informed by his wide-ranging and open-minded studies in the wisdom of *both* East and West. This has not been narrowly confined to the religious sphere either; Phiroz Mehta has a remarkable and up-to-date knowledge of science, philosophy, music and a great deal else besides. A brief scan of the bookshelves in his library reveals brightly covered modern paperbacks by Fritjof Capra (himself at one time a fairly frequent visitor at Forest Hill), Prof. David Bohm, Carl Sagan and Ken Wilber sitting alongside more venerable tomes by G. R. S. Mead (the remarkable Theosophical writer), Krishnamurti of course, Madame Blavatsky, Darwin, Teilhard de Chardin, D. T. Suzuki, Dr I. B. Horner and Edward Conze; numerous classic texts (Plato, Aristotle, the Vedas, the Upanishads, Pali Text Society editions of Buddhist *suttas*); works on Kabbalah, Judaism, Christianity, Quantum Physics, History, Modern European Philosophy . . . Though he never had a personal guru and on the whole kept a certain distance from even the best spiritual groups, Phiroz Mehta has benefited from a close association with many fine minds. In particular in 1963 he was privileged to receive four days' personal instruction in Mahayāna Buddhism from H.H. the Dalai Lama.

•

All these influences have gone into the melting-pot, or perhaps better, the alchemical crucible, out of which Phiroz Mehta has extracted the refined gold of his own writings and teachings. But we must mention another vital ingredient too: his own experience in striving to live the *brahmacarīya*, the holy life. This is most important; mere book learning is not sufficient. Many people can write knowledgeably and inspiringly about spiritual matters; comparatively few are able to live out what they know and write. In this existential respect, as a living exemplar of the *brahmacarīya*, lies Phiroz Mehta's true greatness.

•

We have collected here the various essays and interviews that Phiroz Mehta contributed over a period of more than thirty years to *The Middle Way*, the quarterly journal of the Buddhist Society. It is a substantial body of work by any standard. Many of the essays were originally lectures delivered under the auspices of the Society, some of them at its annual Summer School, held until recently at High Leigh, a great house near Hoddesden in Hertfordshire, where for many years Phiroz Mehta conducted a regular week-long class in the Oak Room. The long and happy association with the Society grew out of a prior association with it Founder/President, the late Christmas Humphreys (1901–83), a contemporary at Cambridge and a lifelong friend and supporter.

•

One thing that is unique about these essays is their freedom from all sectarianism and divisiveness, traditionally aspects of the shadow side of religious life in the West and sadly already beginning to blight the current transmission of the Eastern religions to this hemisphere. At the high point from which Phiroz Mehta writes, at the very frontiers of the ineffable, all differences, comparisons and value judgements fall away. Here the prophets of Israel, the *rishis* of the Vedas and the Upanishads, and great yogis like the incomparable Yājñavalkya rub shoulders with the likes of Gautama the Buddha, Jesus Christ and Jalāluddin Rūmī.

•

What happy consonance reigns among these great spirits! And so it should, for in them the personal had been replaced by the transpersonal. It was their followers who systematized their teachings, and then quibbled and battled over which was right and best, which wrong and damnable. Spiritual truth is the work of the great ones; conventional religious formulations are the creations of lesser men. Even today the orthodox Buddhist will trot out his standard criticism that the benighted Vedic and Upanishadic teachers (whom of course he has never actually read) propounded an erroneous Soul View (*Ātman* Doctrine), whereas the enlightened Buddhists, on the other hand, got it right with a Not-soul View (*anattā* or *anātman* doctrine). Phiroz Mehta, equally at home and sympathetic to Veda, Upanishad and Sutta, can show that, at the highest levels, when say Yājñavalkya spoke of *ātman*, his view was quite consistent with Siddhartha Gautama's view of *anātman*. And moreover he does this, not by boiling everything down to a common broth, but by fully appreciating and even celebrating the singularity of these great teachers.

•

In an age which extols speed and quick results, Phiroz Mehta in these essays offers timely warnings against attempting to force the pace of spiritual progress. It is a natural unfolding; it wants and needs to happen; but the correct conditions must be present. So often, though, we prefigure the end result and then try to contrive it by resorting to forceful techniques, of which so many, once closely guarded secrets, are now being openly peddled in the contemporary spiritual supermarket. Absolutely vital is a moral basis: without this, anything that is achieved is certain to miscarry, perhaps disastrously. Repeatedly, Phiroz Mehta exhorts us to cultivate the traditional virtues.

•

As for meditation, this is not emphasized as a self-conscious mechanical practice to be performed at set times, etc.; rather what is important is the continuous application of close, dispassionate attention. This is very near to, if not identical with, Krishnamurti's *choiceless awareness*. We should attend closely to all that happens, neither being drawn to it (desire) nor pushing it away (aversion). Not least, this will help us to know ourselves —and particularly important in the early stages is *understanding our own motivation*. For almost invariably our initial efforts in the spiritual sphere are grounded in extremely self-centred impulses—ambition, the desire for power or the bliss of trance states, etc. We cannot, however, expunge these and instantly substitute right motives, but under the spotlight of close and constant awareness, conducted on a proper moral basis, they will wither away naturally. Watchfulness and morality are therefore the trusty guardians of the Way.

•

Attention will also bring us into stark confrontation with the dark side of ourselves: the devil within whose unwelcome face we usually project outwards onto some hapless scapegoat. Phiroz Mehta reminds us of the Christian dictum: '*Resist not evil*'. It cannot be safely suppressed or spirited away. Watchfulness will keep it in check, however—and as for the devil: we can only strive to make friends with him. Then, he will gradually be transformed.

•

Like Krishnamurti, Phiroz Mehta stresses the importance of freedom in the living of the *brahmacarīya*, for each individual is a unique creation of the primordial creative energy and his/her flowering can only happen in its own unique way; rigid rules or régimes will merely cramp or distort the process. On the other hand, this freedom must be a disciplined one; it must not be allowed to degenerate into mere licence.

•

Phiroz Mehta is unequivocal about one thing: there is nothing for *me* in living the religious life. How can there be, for what is involved is a progress from selfishness to true selflessness. And when the purity of perfect selflessness is achieved, then the individual human body assumes its rightful condition as a temple to accommodate the divine presence. When this happens, what he calls *holistic consciousness* is established: a non-separative, all-inclusive consciousness that recognises the interconnectedness and hence the essential unity of all and everything. The establishment of this can never be a personal achievement; quite the contrary, the personal is set completely aside and Totality reaps the reward.

•

In this book, then, lies spiritual vision of the first order; inspired writing and impeccable scholarship too. Here also the reader will find sound advice from one who has actually striven to lead the holy life as a householder amidst the hurly-burly of modern urban life. For all of us struggling on the Path in the unpropitious circumstances of the contemporary world, falling by the wayside from time to time, exhausted, dispirited, it is inspiring to know, despite our blackest periodic fears to the contrary, that *'It can still be done'*!

John Snelling
Sharpham
March 1988

That Brāhman, the Buddha

(1954)

> *Monks, I am a Brāhmin, one to ask a favour of . . . Ye are my own true sons, born of my mouth, born of Dhamma, my spiritual heirs.*
>
> (Itivuttaka, 4. 1. 1.)

IN THE GOSPEL of St Luke (3. 23-38), a line of ascent is traced from Jesus right up to Adam. If we turn to Genesis, we find that God creates Adam in his own likeness. Adam, at the age of 130, it is alleged, begets Seth in his own likeness; Seth at the age of 105, it is alleged, begets Enos in his own likeness. From the time of Enos, men begin to call upon the name of the Lord. Enos, at 90, begets Cainan, and so the line goes on to Noah, who is apparently a mature 500 before the arrival of Shem, Ham and Japheth. It comes to pass when men begin to multiply on earth, and daughters are born unto them, that the sons of God, seeing that the daughters of men are fair, take them as wives, as many as they choose. To them, children are born. These become mighty men of renown, true heroes. But God sees that great is the wickedness of man, that every thought of his heart is evil. Then comes the Flood. It is commonly regarded as a flood of destruction—or was it, in reality, a flood of purification? But since Noah walked with God, he found grace in the eyes of the Lord. So too, earlier, Enoch had walked with God. And it is said of Enoch that he was not, for God took him, whereas it is said of all the others that they lived so many years and then died. More than two thousand years later, Elijah is transported by a whirlwind to heaven in a chariot of fire. Almost another millennium swings past, and there takes place the resurrection of Jesus.

Just as there is a line of ascent traced from Jesus to God, so too in the *Brihad-Āraṇyaka Upanishad,* which is at least seven or eight centuries earlier than the time of St Luke, a line of ascent is traced from Pautimāshya to Brahman Svayambhū, Self-existent God.

Adam and Eve are called the first parents. So too, in the Iranian tradition, Yima and his sister-spouse Yimak are called the parents of the first mortals. Like Adam, Yima too falls from grace. Just as Enoch and Elijah are credited with not dying, so too in the Iranian tradition, Kai-Kushro, one of the great king-sages, retires from the world and, immortal, awaits the day of return to rule over a world wherein righteousness shall have triumphed. Immortal, too, is the great priest, the Dastur Paishotan. Even as Jesus spells redemption from Adam's sin, Zarathushtra heals the deadly wound of Yima's self-pride.

But, in the Rig Vedic tradition, there is no fall from grace by Yama and his sister-spouse Yamī. Yama, it is said, chooses death and abandons his body, passes to the other world and is given lordship over the highest of the three heavens. He becomes the Lord of Death, that is the Master of Death, not to be confused with Mrityu or Māra the death-dealer. Yama is the first man to win immortality. Again, the great Rig Vedic *rishis,* those sacred singers of the song of eternal life, see the gods, communicate with them and are at home with them even as Adam and his generations and all the prophets of Israel are at home with the Lord.

What does it all mean? To this day there are prophets, there are *munis,* there are those who are at home with God. But you will not find them among the haunts of men, or at least you will not easily find them unless you have the trained eye with which to see. Since the old days, centuries and millennia have flowed by. Theologians and philosophers of religion have piled system upon system, like bundle upon bundle of cut grass making a haystack. The heavy voice of orthodoxy is too much like the voice of one in a stupor, laden with the burden of mere learning. Those whose cold, black light of intellect is unredeemed by insight flounder about with their ideas like fish caught in a net. Whilst the voracious intellect, gorged on a surfeit of hard facts, spews out its mountains of verbiage, the Book of Life gets buried deeper and deeper under the gathering dust of knowledge. The eyes of God meanwhile moisten as the cloud of unknowing is thickened to an almost impenetrable fog.

And yet, not just there but *here*, not just yesterday or tomorrow but *now* is the incarnate truth. Not lost in the temporal movement of the space-time world but poised *here—now* in fulfilment in eternal existence; this is the meaning of it all, the activity which brings all manifestation to fruition in terms of eternal beauty, the supreme possibility of the realization of the consciousness of the kingdom of heaven, of Brahman-knowing, of Nirvana. And all this is for you *here-now*. It is yours. Take it. You are free. And if you can't take it, it means that you are not free, and all your vaunted individuality and self-determination and democracy are a fantastic make-believe, hurtful to your neighbour and to yourself.

Come with me on a fascinating journey.

Once upon a time, before Adam walked in his garden, there was a group of people whose sense of wonder deepened as they grew older. They were touched with the dissatisfaction engendered by the cycle of birth and death. They yearned for an indefinable fulfilment of their lives. And they considered the question of sorrow. How endless and meaningless seemed the round of uprising-proceeding-dying, uprising-proceeding-dying! How tormenting, how infuriatingly restrictive! Was there an escape from it? An escape which would spell immortality *here-now*, ineffable peace and the certitude that *this-all* was worthwhile? Or was immortality reserved for the gods alone, or maybe for some over-God, miserable autocrat over gods and men?

So these men brooded, seeking the significance of all experience, seeking the eternal creative fount of all existence. And when they died, as indeed each and every single body dies never to resurrect again, their disciples continued to seek. And they discovered that the more they discarded all their preconceptions and vain beliefs, the more they cultivated continual mindfulness, the more they understood themselves and tamed and trained themselves, the nearer they approached their goal. This goal could not be easily defined—to this day it cannot be clearly defined—*but it could be fully experienced.* These men discovered that in the effort to hold the mind still, guarded, deliberately abstracted from the impact of the world on the senses, a new awareness of existence began to emerge and a profounder understanding of certain matters was obtained through concentrated attention.

Now, as one enters profounder states of consciousness, if the next succeeding stage cannot be successfully reached the practitioner may return to ordinary consciousness. This is what most people do. If a person is already in one of the deeper states of consciousness and cannot deliberately go deeper, he may fall asleep, as did the disciples of Jesus in the Garden of Gethsemane; or, if he loses control, but not seriously, he may 'see' visions and 'hear' messages; or, if he loses control to a serious extent, he may become obsessed—possessed of a devil, as happened in the New Testament—which is a very sorry condition; or, he may go off into a deep trance in which a partly healing, whole-making or integrative process goes on. He is unaware of the process, but enjoys the fruit of it—and not all of it is beneficial—on returning to ordinary consciousness.

Adam was the first (or one among the very earliest) of the human race to go off into such a deep trance. That is the so-called sleep that the Lord God causes to fall upon him. On waking up, he finds Eve, fully formed, which means that he becomes clearly conscious of his own psyche, and especially of the feminine aspect complementing his normal masculinity. But what is far more important than this is that Adam is convinced of unitary selfhood and of the unity of the universe. From this is born the conviction, and the consequent teaching, that there is only the one God: a conviction which scatters the host of many gods. Their ephemeral day is over; they disappear like moths devoured by a flame.

But Adam's conviction is not a full and true realization. He has not sufficient self-knowledge and self-discipline to prevent his own fall. Unable to maintain the consequences in daily life of the consciousness of unitary God, his awareness sinks back to the level of the circle of mortality. This is the eating of the fruit of the tree of the knowledge of good and evil. So, in the cool of the evening (classically the time for prayer or meditation: for restoring the deeper states of consciousness), the Lord God, as it is said in Genesis, asks, 'Where art thou, Adam?' meaning, to what level has your consciousness sunk?

Physically, Adam lives a normal human length of life, not 930 years as said in the Bible. About 130 years after Adam, Seth arises. He is developed enough to succeed to the mastership vacated by Adam. That is the meaning of Adam begetting Seth in his own likeness at the age of 130. Adam's teaching flourishes for about a millennium. That is the meaning of all the days of Adam being 930 years. But when the seventh successor to Adam appears on the scene, the deepest depth of consciousness is touched, for Enoch realizes immortality *here-now* in full Superconsciousness. That is the meaning of the statement, 'Enoch was not, for God took him.' The body of Enoch unquestionably died, like any other body dies.

At this point let us turn to Yama of the Vedic tradition. Yama, it is said, chooses death; that is, he frees himself from all bondage to the sensuous life and worldly values. He clearly understands that the cycle of birth and death, *saṃsāra,* is really the stream of consciousness: of emotions and thoughts as they arise-proceed-die, arise-proceed-die, unbidden. He learns in meditation to enter profounder states of consciousness and to master the unbidden flow of discursive thought. At last he is able, in full self-possession, to die altogether to worldly consciousness; that is, to completely stop the flow of discursive thought. This is the meaning of Yama abandoning his body and passing to the inner world. The inner world is not the world of discursive thought, however profound, nor the world of trances, nor of the visions or ecstasies of the saints. All these belong to the sphere of the mortal, for they are all constituted of uprising-proceeding-dying. But when, fully conscious, the flow of discursive thought is completely stopped, deliberately, then there is no uprising-proceeding-dying. This is Superconsciousness, which functions in terms of 'As it was in the beginning is now and ever shall be', in full simultaneity or wholeness; and this, wherein all discursive thought is completely stilled and all birth and death transcended, is the full experience and meaning of immortality. Immortality is the experience of a mode of functioning of consciousness: a mode distinguishing so remarkable a state of consciousness that we may well call it Superconsciousness. Time and space (the condition of bodily being), pain and pleasure (the touchstone of our psycho-physical life) and good and evil as we know them here are all transcended; and you eat of the fruit of the Tree of Life.

This attainment of Superconsciousness is the meaning of Yama being granted lordship over the highest of the three heavens and becoming the Lord of Death.

Whoever attains Superconsciousness is a true fount and source of religion. The attainment of Superconsciousness, which is the experience of the Silence, the Void, the Plenum, the Infinite, the Absolute, is the source-experience from which have emerged the teachings embodied in words like Brahman, Ātman, Iśvara, Godhead, God, Eternity, Immortality, Nirvana, the Kingdom of Heaven, etc.

The *Atharva Veda* (XI. 5. 5.) says:

> The Brahmachārī, earlier born than Brahmā,
> sprang up through fervour, robed in hot libation;
> From him sprang heavenly lore, the highest Brahmā,
> and all the gods, with life that lasts for ever.

And again:

> Therefore, whoever knoweth man, regardeth him as Brahman's self,
> For all the deities abide in him, as cattle in their pen.
>
> (XI. 8. 32.)

Amongst that host of sacred singers of the song of eternal life, the great *rishis* who composed the hymns of the *Rig Veda*, must be numbered the true *munis* who realized the meaning of Silence and experienced immortality here-now. The *Rig Veda* says (VIII. 48. 3.):

> We have drunk Soma and become immortal;
> We have attained the light, the gods discovered.

Therefore, it is very sad when anyone, spiritually dulled by the weight of mere learning, misleads those who seek Truth, by declaring that the *Vedas*, or indeed any of the great scriptures of the ancient world, were mere guesses at truth or gropings after reality by a primitive people in their spiritual infancy. It is those who have not attained Superconsciousness, or who have no intuitive insight into the significance of the Silence, the Plenum, who spin out those doctrines and dogmas, often at variance amongst themselves, which bind man to the circle of mortality whilst paying lip-service to Immortal God, and which thereby confuse people with regard to the nature of the transcendent consummation towards which they are developing.

The realization of Superconsciousness cannot be spun out into philosophic systems. Only a few statements can be made, which may inspire others to seek or sustain those who are already searching. This realization of Superconsciousness is the full and true meaning of the Upanishadic phrases, 'realizing the Ātman', knowing 'Brahman' and 'having ascended aloft, he became immortal'. That *yogeśvara*, Yājñavalkya, price of yogis, declared in the *Brihad-Āraṇyaka Upanishad* (III. 8. 10):

> Verily, O Gārgī, he who departs from this world
> without knowing that Imperishable, is pitiable;
> But, O Gārgī, he who departs from this world
> knowing that Imperishable is a *brāhman*.

'Departs from this world' is usually understood as bodily death, but in this context there is a more profound meaning: entry into deeper states of consciousness. As explained earlier, if there is loss of control in the process, one may fall asleep or go off into a trance and so forth, in which case one 'departs from this world' without knowing the Deathless. But he who can successfully make the final grade and stop the flow of discursive thought, deliberately and in full conscious control of the situation, he indeed knows the Deathless on 'departing from this world'.

Listen again to Yājñavalkya (IV. 4. 14):

> Verily, while we are here we may know this.
> If you have known it not, heavy is the loss.
> Those who know this become immortal,
> But others go only to sorrow.

So we see that a real *brāhman* is one who knows that Imperishable, knows Brahman, and who can be at home in that silence which is the immortal Superconsciousness of eternal existence. The *Mundaka Upanishad* says (III. 2. 9):

> He, verily, who knows that supreme Brahman becomes very Brahman . . . He crosses over sin, he crosses over sorrow . . . Liberated from the knots of the heart, he becomes immortal.

The true *brāhman*, then, is one who has become Brahman. Answering the question, 'Who indeed is a *brāhman?*', the *Vajrasūchī Upanishad* tells us that whosoever a man may be,

> He who has directly realized the Ātman,
> who is directly cognizant of the Ātman,
> . . . which cannot be reasoned about but is
> known only by direct cognition . . .
> he alone is a *brāhman*.

At its very heart, then, the teaching of the great *rishis* and *munis*, of all the great spiritual teachers, as enshrined in *Veda* and *Upanishad*, *Gītā* and *Gāthā*, *Sutta* and Bible, is the teaching about Superconsciousness, called Brahman-knowing or God-realization, and about the Path which leads to the realization of the immortal *here-now*. At its very heart, all true religion is concerned with bringing a man to full fruition, first in terms of character—the perfected man, the exemplar, and next in terms of the realization of Superconsciousness.

Now let us turn to Canto 26 of the *Dhāmmapada*:

> (1) O *brāhman,* struggle hard; dam the torrent of craving and drive away sensual pleasures. When thou hast understood how to root out the elements of being, then, O *brāhman,* wilt thou realize the Uncreated.
>
> (3) He for whom exist neither the six internal nor the six external states of consciousness, nor both; he who is free and fearless, him I call a *brāhman.*

'Free and fearless'—*free* to attain Superconsciousness by entering the deeper states of consciousness one by one, and finally stopping the flow of discursive thought; and *fearless,* because it requires unusual courage to take the plunge into the Void, for there is no knowing what may happen.

> (29) Him I call a *brāhman* in whom there exists no craving; who has reached correct understanding; who is free from doubt and who has plumbed the depths of the Immortal.

'Free from doubt'—*doubt* that the silence is the fullness, is the Superconsciousness; the fearful mind of him who is confined within the sphere of mortality is inclined to believe that the stopping of the flow of discursive thought merely means emptiness, vacuity.

In Canto 10 we have this verse:

> (6) If, like a shattered gong, thou hast learnt Silence, thou hast already reached Nirvana––there is no anger within thee.

Look through the pages of the Buddha's discourses, and you will find again and again the Buddha's statements concerning the entering into profounder states of consciousness, culminating in what he calls the stopping of feeling, knowing and perception, which I describe as the stopping at will of the flow of discursive thought. The Buddha himself achieved this Superconsciousness and could enter it as and when he pleased and remain in it as long as he pleased. This attainment, which is the same as the Upanishadic 'knowing Brāhman' or 'realizing the ātman' or 'ascending aloft and becoming immortal', is precisely the very heart of the enlightenment of the Buddha. So on the way to Gayā, the Buddha says to Upaka:

> The Arahant am I, teacher supreme,
> Utter Enlightenment is mine alone;
> Unfever'd calm is mine, Nirvana's peace.
> I seek the Kāśis's city, there to start
> my Doctrine's wheel, a purblind world to save,
> sounding the tocsin's call to Deathlessness.

When he first addresses, in the deer park of Isipatana, the five who were to be his first disciples, he categorically assures them:

> The Immortal is found. I instruct, I teach the Doctrine. Going along in accordance with what is enjoined, having soon realized here and now by your own superknowledge that supreme goal of the Brahma-faring . . . you will abide in it.

Siddhattha Gotama, in becoming the all-enlightened Buddha, had also become the true *brāhman*: one who had become Brahman. The venerable *bhikkhu*, Kaccāna the Great, declared (*M*. I. 111.):

> The Lord has become vision, become knowledge, become *dhamma*, become Brahmā; he is the propounder, the expounder, the bringer to the goal, the giver of the Deathless, *dhamma*-lord, Tathāgata.

In the *Agganna Sutta*, the Buddha himself declares (D. 3. 84):

> Vāseṭṭha, these are names tantamount to Tathāgata; belonging to the *dhamma*, and again belonging to Brahmā; and again, *dhamma*-become, and again Brahma-become.

And it is significant that the Buddha declares this immediately after saying:

> He, Vāseṭṭha, whose faith in the Tathāgata is settled, rooted, established and firm, not to be dragged down by anyone, well may he say, 'I am a veritable son of the Exalted One.'

I leave it to you to think of the use of the word 'son' in this statement by the Buddha in relation to the use of the word 'son' in the genealogy in St Luke's Gospel from Jesus to God.

That *brāhman*, the Buddha, was one of the supreme heirs and noblest representatives of the profoundest religious development the world has ever seen. As the young seeker of truth, he saw suffering around him, suffering as we ordinarily understand it. As the all-enlightened Brahma-become Buddha of his maturity, he saw suffering, *dukkha*, everywhere and in everything, including what we commonly regard as good and worthwhile. But *this dukkha, this* ill-state, meant something infinitely profounder than sickness, old age, infirmity, heartbreak and all the ephemeral ills of this world. This *dukkha* meant absence of permanent Nirvana; absence of that *upekkhā* which is the dynamic poise that knows no shaking; absence of that absolute freedom of mind which is won through the perfecting of character and of clear-visioned insight; absence of the power to stop at will the flow of discursive thought and enter Superconsciousness. It was this *dukkha* from which the Buddha found and taught the way of deliverance. This suffering as taught by the Buddha is identical with the Upanishadic anguish of separation from the *Tad-va-nam*, the goal of love-longing, which is Brahman the Immortal Beloved. And in both cases, the transcending of this anguish, which is the realization of Brahman by a *muni*, or Nirvana by a Buddha, is the realization of Superconsciousness.

The master who experiences the immortal in Superconsciousness naturally and inevitably teaches his disciples that that is the true goal of the spiritual life. Equally naturally and inevitably, those who seek the immortal ask questions and await answers regarding the nature of this goal. But questions and answers, framed in words which express thoughts, all arise and are confined to the sense-mind sphere, which is the sphere of uprising-proceeding-dying, the sphere of mortality. The terms and criteria of the sphere of mortality and of separate entity or diversity do not properly apply to the sphere of immortality and eternal existence, which is that of unity. So, the inadequacy of the mortal inevitably distorts the as-it-really-is-ness of the immortal. Human beings, with minds confined to the sphere of mortality, easily conceive of a god in their own image, exalted to a superlative degree. But this god, as an entity, and with man-bestowed qualities, is a strange idol, a grey image of the unimaginable reality . . . unimaginable, that is, but fully realizable in Superconsciousness. When mortals say that their teacher is the Son of God, one with God, etc., they are talking devoutly; but there is a considerable measure of misconception in what they say. Again, those who spin out theologies which purport, sincerely enough, to make plain the eternal light, do in fact cast fantastic shadows whilst trying to utilize that light. You cannot use the light of truth for your own purposes. You can only *become* the light: *be enlightened.* And only he with a pure heart can clearly see that light. If and when he who has attained uses terms like *Brahman, God, Eternity, Nirvana,* etc., he knows what he is talking about, for the meaning of those terms is an actual blissful inward realization; whereas for him who has not realized the silence, the meaning of those terms is an externalized product of his imagination.

Fully understanding the difficulty, almost the impossibility, of containing the unconditioned Immortal within the strangely fashioned cup of restrictive speech-thought, the great *munis* and teachers, *arahants* and buddhas refused to be professional theologians. Instead, they demonstrated in their own everyday lives the consequence of their Brahman-becoming. They taught the way of life which leads to the realization *here-now* of eternal life: the way which transforms a man into a true *brāhman.*

It is particularly significant that the last canto of the *Dhammapada* is called the 'Canto of the *Brāhman*', and the refrain, 'Him I call a *brāhman*' is used in no less than thirty-two verses to describe the person who has trod the steps of the Noble Eightfold Path and attained supreme Nirvana.

Some 5,000 years and more have passed since the days when Enoch walked with God, days which may perhaps coincide with the days when Yama chose death and abandoned his body, entered the inner world and was granted lordship over the highest of the three heavens. With the passing of the centuries, the great *rishis* and *munis* of ancient India handed down their treasured wisdom of the way of deliverance and of the holy experience of immortality in Superconsciousness to their disciples, their 'sons of proven worth'. That holy experience they termed *Brahman-knowing*: crossing over sorrow, crossing over sin, liberation from the knots of the heart. In the course of a millennium or so, theologies and strange theories began to appear. Theologies and theories are the sport of the not fully enlightened servants of the intellect, the unenlightened monarchs of mere verbiage. And when the truth of the way of deliverance was in danger of submergence, Gotama the Buddha came to wrest immortality from the very jaws of Māra the death-dealer. The Buddha gave a fresh emphasis to the practical aspects of treading the perfect way; and he and his *aryan bhikkhus* did not cloister themselves in one place for their lifetime, but moved from town to town and village to village.

More than 2,400 years have gone by since the Buddha uttered his last words: 'Strive on with diligence.' The face of the world has undergone remarkable change. Great deeds and terrible deeds have been done. Knowledge has piled up mountainously. But the fevered heart of man is still restless, questing for the end of his anguish, questing for the goal of his love-longing. Man professes disillusionment today, puts on the mask of obstinate incredulity and plays at being objective and scientific, matter-of-fact and rational. But life will sweep away all his professions and pretensions in her irresistible tide, for ultimately man must come to the light, even if the only path left to him is through the portals of death.

Do you look, then, for some petty consolation? Do you await some futile message of hope? Let it be clearly realized that in the transcendent awareness of eternal existence there is no room and no meaning for either hope or despair, pessimism or optimism. *Here-now* is the ultimate, the supreme, for we continually exist in the very midst of the omnipresent, and there is not a secret of the heart which is hidden from the gaze of the eyes which never sleep.

So the question is, Adam, where do you *want* to be? At home in omniscience, bending every energy in harmony with omnipotence; or, buffeted between the extremes of the dualistic temporal, the miserable slave of savage folly?

In this century, *here, now,* it is the springtime of the spirit once again. And it is also the harvest-time of the spirit. This simultaneity of spring-time and harvest is the sign and miracle for our day. And he who is ready or who will diligently prepare himself will be an active participator in this miracle and not a mere blind spectator.

Once again the portals are open through which have constantly passed the great religious heroes—the prophets of old, *rishis* and *munis, arahants* and buddhas; a wonderful company of perfected men, the Brahman-become, among whom shines the overtowering figure of that *brāhman,* the Buddha.

What do we Seek?

(1962)

IT IS NECESSARY to enquire, *What do we seek in life? What is our objective? What do the millions seek?* And if we look around, we cannot fail to see that people seek excitement and sensational pleasures, family and home, property and wealth, the fulfilment of political, professional and social ambitions, security and success, cultural advancement and spiritual growth.

What is the aim of it all? In human terms, we say happiness or the fulfilment of life. When these human terms are taken to their highest level, we use religious terms like the Kingdom of Heaven, as the Christian would say; or *Moksha* (Liberation), as the Hindu would say; or Nirvana, as the Buddhist would say.

A great teacher said:

> Peace I leave with you; my peace I give unto you: not as the world giveth, give I unto you.
> Let not your heart be troubled, neither let it be fearful.
>
> JOHN xiv, 27

The different forms of happiness sought depend upon a person's age and circumstances and character. The form sought by the religious is peace, and this indeed is the form offered by the great teachers.

We must note carefully that this peace is not the peace which the world gives. The worldly meaning of peace is far distant from the peace attained by the great teachers. To glimpse the spiritual meaning of peace, we must remember the Buddha's teaching that greed, hate and delusion, and all the ill brood born of those three, are great hindrances to anyone striving to tread the path to peace.

Discipline is indispensable for winning freedom from these hindrances. Essentially, this discipline consists of the purification of the mind and heart through meditation and constant mindfulness. Meditation is not mere musing or an inconsequential rambling of the mind. That way lies intellectual dissipation and mental debauchery. Meditation is concentrated attentiveness upon the matter in hand, *here-now*. What is ordinarily and in its own context correctly called the active life is thus only a small part of the total activity, physical and mental, of the meditator. For the true meditator performs all actions mindfully; he or she thinks and feels and speaks mindfully.

This mindful, silent observation of the entire becoming-process is carried out without taking sides for or against. When freed of all aversion or attraction and of all blame or praise as a mere reaction to that which is observed, mindfulness acts as a power to *dis*-solve all those expressions of our physical energy which we describe as lust, anger and so forth, and then to *re*-solve that liberated energy into forms which are greedless, hateless and so forth. Meditation is therefore a kind of alchemy, and the concentrated attentiveness with which we dispassionately watch the becoming-process is an instrument of purification or transmutation.

All this sounds very strenuous. Yes it is, and further, it is a work for one's whole lifetime. But who would be so foolish as to hope to run a four-minute mile by ambling round the back-garden on Sunday mornings—be the ambling ever so religious!

And yet, spiritual growth is marked by the resolution of paradoxical opposites. Be *gently* strenuous, and we realize a small degree of ease. Be *fully* strenuous, and complete ease is ours.

Take the playing of the piano. Practise half an hour a day, and we can entertain our friends after dinner with some pleasant music. Practise ten hours a day and, granted the gift of the gods is there to start with, we could be inspired and inspiring concert artists. But the outstanding characteristic of the concert artist's performance is that it seems—and indeed is—so effortless. Listen to a superb pianist play a slow movement (and a *slow* movement is the supreme test) by a consummate musical craftsman like Mozart! The effortless performance and ease of creative re-creation are the fruit of endless, painstaking, concentrated attention and practice.

So too, constant mindfulness and persuasive, friendly self-control lead to the end of greed, hate and delusion, to the end of *dukkha*; and they bear fruit as vision, as gleams of the light of the transcendent which gather into the full splendour of enlightenment and as the peace which is Nirvana. Suffice it to mention just that. The full fruit is beyond description—and is indeed of the rarest savour in silence alone.

'You Talk—I Listen'

(1964)

A BABEL of discordant voices murders peace:

'I am an immortal soul . . .' 'I am a spark of God . . .' 'The body dies but my real Self goes on . . .' 'I am just this body and death means the end of all of me . . .' 'I am born over and over again until I reach salvation and finally rest in Nirvana . . .' 'I have only one life to live in this world and salvation can be won only through the grace of God'—and so on and on.

But he who will sit at ease by the still waters and listen to the voice of the silence may meet the Beloved and realize the Deathless. There is no one here insensible to the cry of suffering. The very pursuit of happiness, of love and of success—and how wild that pursuit is!—proclaims the emptiness of the heart. Look with a compassionate eye and see the distress of the mind battling with the why and the wherefore of existence, with the problems of evil and of death. And who can fail to see the grim lordship of death? And what after death? An infinite dreary repetition of births that end only in death? Or is there a ray of light to feed hope?

But first taste more suffering, and still more till there be no more suffering upon which to feed. Life cannot be bypassed by means of the treachery of consolatory fantasies posing as truth. Therefore listen in uttermost quiet and hear the soul of Mother Earth crying to Father Heaven that she can no longer bear the pain of man's iniquity. Hear her crying for the fearless, invincible hero who will deliver her. Listen we must and with reverence, for we are the issue from earth's side through heaven's alchemy. And the assuaging of earth's pain also spells our own healing. Listen again and hear the cry of the Son of Man, self-exiled from his home of splendour, the eternal light, suffering existence here in this realm of mortality, dominated by the Lord of Death.

And yet it was the will of the Supreme that sowed man into the cosmos: a seed of unimaginable promise, predestined to blossom into divine fulfilment. Speaking to his disciple, his son Tat, Hermes Trismegistus says that this seed is the true good and that the matter and the womb out of which man is born is the wisdom that listens in silence. The will of the Supreme then sowed man into the cosmos. This action is karma. Not understanding karma, unaligned with perfect action, man performs actions which produce suffering. But the divine action is the great sacrifice, the prototype of the ritual worship.

When Arjuna asks Sri Krishna, 'What is karma?' the incarnate Lord of the Universe answers, 'That emanantion of Brahman which causes the creation of beings is action.' Uddālaka Aruni, who uttered the great teaching *tat twam asi* ('That Thou Art'), tells Yājñavalkya that once when he was studying the sacrifice he came to know Brahman the Supreme.

This sacrifice, this action, this karma, goes on perpetually, or else the world would fall into ruin, as Sri Krishna declared. Even as the Upanishadic teachers spoke of Brahman the Supreme, Thrice Greatest Hermes spoke of God. In the Hermetic teachings, the Supreme declares to the initiate after granting him a vision, 'That Light am I, thy God, Mind. The Logos, the emanation of Mind, is the son of God. The vision of Me which thou seest in thy mind is thy archetypal form whose being is before beginning and without end.' And he goes on to teach 'and God the Mind, being male and female, both as light and life subsisting, brought forth another mind, and this other mind formed seven rulers who enclose the Cosmos that the senses perceive. But All-Father mind being light and life did bring forth man, co-equal to himself, with whom he fell in love, as being his own child, for he was beautiful beyond compare, the image of his sire. In very truth God fell in love with his own form and on him did bestow all his own formations. After man-the-image-of-God-the-mind, had learned the essence and become a sharer of the nature of the seven rulers, he desired to break through the boundary of the cosmos, the ring-pass-not, and subdue the might of that which pressed upon the fire here below, a creative energy of the material world. So when he presented himself, the divine form of perfect beauty, nature, smiling with love, wound herself completely round him, and he, beholding the form like unto himself reflected in the water of nature, loved it, willed to live in it and thus vivified the material form devoid of reason. Hence above all creatures on earth man is two-fold. Mortal because of the body, immortal because of the essential man.'

The Buddha also speaks of the essential man, *sato sattassa*, and declares emphatically that he has not taught the destruction of this essential man. The Hermetic teachings say further: 'Though deathless and possessed of sway over all, yet does he suffer as a mortal doth, subject to fate.' This 'suffering as a mortal doth', is karma in the sphere of mortality. This is the lesser karma, karma as equilibration, karma as the continuous emergence of the new situation, somewhat inadequately described as cause-and-effect. But when the mortal man here links himself with his divine prototype through fervent aspiration or the height of self surrendering devotion, through the light of wisdom which has penetrated into the beyond, or by a religious rite in which he actually reaches into the great sacrifice, or by the deliberate entry into the supreme ecstatic states in that profound contemplation which is perfect communion, then mortal man here performs the transcendent karma which wipes out a myriad sins and presses himself and all creation closer to the heart of the divine. This is the high office of the priest initiate, of the perfect holy one, of the true teacher.

A mortal's capacity to do this is very limited. How has man here fallen from his God-like estate? How has man, the image of his Father God, Mind, changed from immortal life to mortal soul, from eternal light to temporal confused mind? In beautiful forms have Plato and

Pythagoras, those great philosopher-initiates of ancient times, handed down the secret tradition. Through the star-encircled solitudes which form the boundary of the cosmos, the ring-pass-not, where the zodiac meets our galaxy, the immortal man, unitary and unconditioned, descends earthwards. In his descent, he, a monad, becomes a dyad. Pythagoras says, symbolically, 'the sphere becomes elongated, like unto an egg or a pine cone.' In his *Timaeus,* Plato teaches that the world-soul and the individual soul are indivisible regarded from the standpoint of the simplicity of their divine nature. When the soul is drawn towards the body it experiences a disturbance because of matter flowing into it. In his *Phaedo,* Plato says that the soul is drawn to the body, staggering with recent intoxication. And a symbol of this mystic secret is that starry cup of Bacchus, the constellation Krater, placed in the expanse between the constellations Leo and Cancer. The intoxication first caused here by the influx of matter causes the loss of memory of our divine origin. Some souls lose their memory more than others; they are more intoxicated. When true memory becomes clouded, fantastic opinions arise and their clash is the cacophony of Babel.

Perhaps we can now discern the sweep of karma. Transcendentally, the divine action, the great sacrifice, is the realm of the immortal, of endless light. There is no good and evil here. In the sphere of mortality, however, the battleground of good and evil, karma in the lesser sense operates. Here, we are the victims of karma and also the ordainers of our own karma. When we have the good sense to alter our sights and steer our course back to our true home, we become the masters of karma, till at last, in the beatitude of ever-present enlightenment, the lesser karma stands still for ever.

The mechanism of the operation of karma is rebirth. Like karma, rebirth has its lesser and greater aspects. Transcendentally, life is everlasting; mind knows no break, no oscillation between seemingly unrelated opposites. In the spheres of mortality, life is in disequilibrium, for here our minds experience a break, the memory of our transcendent origin is lost and we wander aimlessly for a long time. But tread the path to liberation and the disequilibrium becomes transformed into the equanimity of harmonious integration. Our mind, attuned to the All Mind, now experiences no break but is fully awake to the continuous emergence of the whole situation through the succession of births and deaths. Bondage to the round of mortality is no more. The lesser rebirth has given place to the greater rebirth, the resurrection and ascension into the transcendent reality. One other greater rebirth there is—the appearance of great teachers who are recognised as divine incarnations (*avatars*).

Love is the motive power of all. If love is merely desire for the things of matter, if it is *taṇhā*, the thirst for sentient existence, then man stays in darkness, whirling in the painful round of *saṃsāra*. But if this love is the will to enlightenment, if it is the true love of God, the irresistible urge for liberation, then man becomes the knower of himself, of himself as he is here, the mortal, and of himself the essential man, the immortal. The thirst for sentient existence is one root cause of *saṃsāra*. The other root cause is the ignorance of the way of home returning, and especially the ignorance of that supreme promise, pregnant in the unequivocal affirmation by the Buddha, that suffering can be extinguished.

What now is *saṃsāra*? Rebirth is most difficult to understand but, if it can be well understood, we hold in our hands a power of knowledge to help us cross over to the blest isle of the deathless. First, some of the names by which *saṃsāra*'s cycle goes—*rebirth, reincarnation, transmigration, metemsomatosis, palingenesis, metempsychosis,* and so on. *Rebirth* will be sufficient for our purposes. Next let us look at some of the obstructions to the understanding of rebirth. These are neatly summed up in the terse perplexity of the statement, 'but I can't remember my past lives': a statement which embodies the two basic problems of memory and personality. With regard to memory, is it not asking too much to remember past lives, when our near past and especially our infancy are too dim to be reliable? And if we cultivate our memory by means of trustworthy disciplines, or if we have memories released by scientific means which take us back as far as our birth or even back into the womb, we come to a full stop with our conception, because we say 'I began when my mother conceived me.'

But how accurate is this statement? Our pronouns, *he, she,* and so on, are convenient words for use in a rough and ready sense only. If it be conceded that the heart in this body be part of me and not of you, then my mother, when the foetus was in her womb, could claim that it was part of her. So too, my father's claim that the fertilizing sperm was part of him would have to be conceded. And if we pursue this line further and further backwards, where would 'I' be then? Where indeed would my father and mother and all my forbears be? *Ah, but you are a separate, distinct individual after parturition.* Am I? When I suckle my mother's breasts, when I drink of a flowing stream, or eat a peach off a tree, or breathe the air here present, is a 'not me' becoming 'me'? Is my son 'me', is his son 'me'? Surely it is clear our pronouns are but convenient linguistic tools. They do not, any more than terms, 'body', 'feeling', 'mind', etc., represent any permanent changeless entity. All the elements composing the human creature, the existential man, are impermanent and in ceaseless flux. Nothing in the empirical context will outlast sufficiently far-reaching analysis. Every single thing dissolves into no-thing, into voidness.

Conversely, out of that very void, out of the no-thing, emerges the thing, the temporary phenomenon. The void is indeed the plenitude. You and I are temporary, mortal, emergences out of the not-temporal, undifferentiated, no-thing. You and I have no absolute beginning or birth, no absolute end or death. There is no absolute *I* or *you* which has a series of lives, each life being regarded as a separate, distinct entity.

And yet this continuous stream of myriads of lives of appearances. Behold the mystery of Maya, the universal play of the void-plenitude pretending to be Reality! And in this play, which goes round and round, each manifestation refers to itself as 'I' and to others as 'they'—unavoidable and useful in the empirical context. And each 'I' in some form or other is ineradicably convinced of its deathlessness, of its indissoluble unity with the transcendent, a conviction indispensable for the dissolution of the ego or the 'I', and its final triumphant at-onement with its immortal source.

Our ordinary feeling of personality, as also of

our self-conception, arises from our conditioning from infancy. Ignorance plays the dominant role here. Freedom from the egoistic misperception of our true being and from the egocentricity of daily living begins when religious discipline enables us to see ourself and all other selves personally, impersonally and trans-personally. Thereby our minds function not only in terms of 'thing' consciousness, which is separative, but also in terms of 'no-thing' consciousness, which correctly relates 'thing' to its original undifferentiation. In the harmony of 'thing' consciousness and 'no-thing' consciousness, we realize the unity of the whole. For then we see the infinite variety of particulars in perfect relationship to each other.

Thus out of the 'no-thing' there emerges the body, out of the void comes the mind. Back to the void go the body and the mind. So we can understand the succession of births and deaths as the patterning and dissipating of material and mental forces in accord with karmic law. The law is quite simple. All the forces at play, material and mental, tend towards a resultant. But to see this patterning and dissipating in its endless variation of detail is too difficult for mortal vision to follow. The pattern is so vast and complicated, human ability so limited.

Let us recall two or three of the statements which have been made in the past regarding what happens after death. A careful consideration of them will indicate why it took me over thirty years to begin to understand rebirth.

Hermes says, 'If the soul persists in vice, it tastes neither the deathless nor the good but speeding back again it turns into the path that leads to creeping things.' He also adds that the soul's vice is ignorance. Its virtue is gnosis, for the good and pious one who knows is already divine while still living in the world. How close all this is to the Indian teachings. For the *Upanishads* also speak of those of evil conduct being reborn as dogs, swine, outcasts and so on. They also speak of the liberated ones while still in the body on earth. In Plato's *Timaeus*, Er the Pamphylian describes his vision where he saw the soul of Telamonian Ajax choose the body of a lion, Agamemnon of an eagle, Atlanta of an athlete, Thersites of an ape. These probably would have to be interpreted symbolically, not literally.

How far the Greeks accepted transmigration and so on we are not quite certain.

But how can we, possessed of the faculties which we have at present, verify such statements for ourselves? For most of us, whirling around in the maelstrom of mortality, rebirth may be intellectually acceptable only as a reasonable theory or it may be implicitly believed in pure faith.

And yet, there is a succession of births and deaths which every one of us experiences here. Throughout our life, from the moment our body is born until the hour of our death, there is a series of states of mind, actions and events, which begin, proceed and pass away. Each has its birth, its little life and its death. We are conscious of this series as a succession of births and deaths. The *Maitri Upanishad* states that, '*Saṃsāra* is just one's own thought . . . By making mind motionless, from sloth and distraction free, when unto mindlessness one comes, then that is the supreme estate' (6. 34); and the *Shandilya Upanishad* also states that, 'When the fluctuations of the mind cease, the cycle of births and deaths comes to an end' (1. 42). This succession is quite easy to see, for there is the linking factor of self-consciousness, 'I am I,' as we say, persisting through the whole series.

But now, what happens to this organic memory, what happens to self-consciousness when the organism dies? It is taught in some of the great religions that the death of the organism spells the obliteration of visual consciousness, tactile consciousness and so on. Organic memory disappears. All that is rooted in the physical senses vanishes. The 'I am I' self-consciousness is utterly wiped out. But it is taught that the overriding mental consciousness, which contains within itself the extracted essence of the total past, persists and carries over into rebirth, although the strands of connection between the death of A and the subsequent birth of B are not visible to us. Can we develop faculties which would enable us to see these threads of connection? Or is there an unusual type of memory which can be awakened, not developed in the way that memory as a faculty of the psycho-physical organism is developed?

The answer to this question takes us into the realm of

the greater rebirth. The discipline of the holy life purifies the mind and the body of the initiate. It develops his power of concentrated attentiveness, undreamed of by any non-practisant of the discipline. It enables him to enter profound modes of consciousness, not open to investigation by the non-practisant, however learned or clever he may be. In these deep modes the yogi or mystic is aware in non-analytical terms. He understands and sees supra-sensually without the use of discursive thought or words. He enters the deep state beyond speech and mind, as the *Upanishads* taught, beyond all feeling and perception, as the Buddha taught, in fully awake, concentrated attentiveness.

This transcendent mode of awareness is the true Super-consciousness in which he whose mortal body is known by a human name has consciously at-oned himself with that essential man, the emanation of mind mentioned earlier. This essential man has been the silent watcher through the ages. The Samkhya teaching of India postulated the *purusha*, this being that is beyond all that can be predicated here. It postulated also *prakriti*, primordial nature. *Purusha* stimulates *prakriti* simply by being the transcendent presence. Then primordial nature stirs and her stirring becomes the awesome and wondrous activity of universal process, whether it be the ring dance of atoms or the outstreaming of stupendous galaxies, the eruption of Erebus or the flowering of a rose, the devilish blackening of a soul or the triumphant ascent into the light of Nirvana. All of it emerges out of primordial nature. When the final disjunction with matter has been realized, the *purusha* is once more itself like the pure essence of mind of Buddhist teaching. This being is the same silent watcher sung also in the *Rig Veda*, and taught in the *Kaṭha*, the *Muṇḍaka* and *Shvetāshvatara Upanishads*. Two birds with fair wings have found a refuge in the same sheltering tree. One of them eats the sweet fig tree's fruit; the other, eating not, looks on. From such holy communion the perfected saint returns to the human plane bringing with him the light and powers of the Supreme, in so far as such powers may function here.

Since the purification of heart and mind is perfect, and concentrated attentiveness in perfect equanimity reaches the depth of freedom from all form, either material or mental, one of those powers is the power to summon before his mind the total past. This is not organic memory where the time factor operates. It is *whole awareness by unified mind.* We can do little more through words than ring a bell in someone who has already had some genuine experience of this as a result of right discipline or by gift of grace. This memory of all the lives is the vision of the total mortal body of appearances with which the transcendent has associated itself. A person's power to do this while living in the body means also the power to relinquish bodily manifestation for ever at will. It also means the power to go through the portals of death in full consciousness. His organic form-dependent memory vanishes but his transcendental recognition of his divine origin comes fully alight. He is indeed the enlightened one. He has refound his pristine divinity. He has at last seen his Original Face.

That concentrated attentiveness, which began as a dim glow enclosed in the mortal vesture of mind and body, now moves out of the last incarnation, out of the boundary, the ring-pass-not, into the splendour and plenitude of boundless light. This greater rebirth which is the ascent into the immortal real is the ultimate fruit of all the suffering in *saṃsāra.*

And he who is reborn into his divine state listening to the cry of the soul of the earth, listening to the cry of suffering humanity, can re-appear in the world to redeem it in the ripeness of the divine circumstance.

The Goal

(1964)

IN THE *Mahāsāropama Sutta*, the Greater Discourse on the Simile of the Pith, the Buddha teaches a group of *bhikkhus* that 'unshakable freedom of mind is the goal, the pith, the culmination of the *brahma*-faring [or treading of the Way].'

He leads up to this affirmation step by step. First, through faith, a man of the world gives up the worldly life and becomes a *bhikkhu*, because he feels that here is a Way, treading which he may become free of the unsatisfactoriness and the anguish of the ordinary, everyday life. After becoming a *bhikkhu*, he receives gains, honours and fame from the lay-folk. But he does not allow himself to get swollen-headed or indolent. Remaining diligent, he progresses on the path and attains 'success in moral habit'. Maintaining his balance, not disparaging others, he proceeds to attain 'success in concentration'. Neither exultant nor slothful, he attains 'knowledge and vision'. At this stage, so the Buddha teaches, he could obtain 'conditional deliverance'. He is like one who has found the pith of the tree. He has right knowledge of the essence of the holy life and could enjoy the fruits thereof. But it is possible to fall away from conditioned freedom. If, however, the *bhikkhu* maintains unflagging diligence, he obtains 'unconditional deliverance'. And it is impossible, declares the Buddha himself, that he should fall away from the emancipation that is timeless.

So the Buddha sums up: 'This brahma-faring is not for

advantage in gains, honours, fame; it is not for advantage in moral habit, nor in concentration, nor in knowledge and vision. But, O *bhikkhus,* that which is unshakable freedom—that is the goal of the brahma-faring, that is the pith, that is the culmination.'

In the next discourse, the *Cūlasāropama Sutta,* the Lesser Discourse on the Simile of the Pith, the Buddha gives the same teaching to a single *brāhman* named Pingalakocca. But after mentioning the stage at which knowledge and vision are attained, the Buddha proceeds to the end of the discourse in a different manner. He asks, 'What are the *dhammā* that are higher and more excellent than knowledge and vision?' And he answers his own question by detailing the four *jhānas* and the four *samāpattis,* which are eight progressively profounder modes of awareness, culminating in a ninth, which is the realization, *here-now,* of Nirvana.

What does all this mean? What are the implications of living the holy life? Let us consider together the stages which are mentioned.

First, the predisposing cause of the turning away from the worldly life: 'I am beset by birth, by ageing and by death. I am beset by suffering, *dukkha,* overwhelmed by suffering.' Beset by birth, ageing and death! Here is the recognition of the tyranny of time, and the acknowledgement that in the sphere of mortality one is like a leaf blown about by a cold autumn wind. Those three words—birth, ageing, death—span the aching distance of only a single stride of the Lord of Death. And so the seeker of the Way cries out that he is overwhelmed by *dukkha.* Here too is the implicit recognition that the Way which leads to the Deathless is the Way to Nirvana. Only when the Deathless is realized will there be the end of *dukkha.* The very word, *dukkha,* basically means 'far from the infinite', or, 'that which spoils (or makes bad) the infinite'. Let us remember that the infinite transcends the duality of birth-death. Also, it is not a mere opposite of birth-ageing-death, for whether the seeker of the Deathless wins it or not, he will unquestionably grow old and die, even as everybody else does.

So we come to the next step. Recognizing that he is overwhelmed by *dukkha*, he turns away from the worldly life and goes forth into the unfamiliar holy life. India has always regarded the devoted effort to live the holy life as more worthy than any other undertaking. Hence, from the laity the *bhikkhu* receives gains, honours and fame. The gains referred to by the Buddha are simply the barest necessities of existence.

Remaining unspoilt by these, he diligently practises *śīla*, the moral precepts. These are not commandments, only advices, with respect to the holy life. If one is earnest about living it, one will find the advices helpful. Nothing is forcibly imposed. But the true disciple regards each and every advice as both law and method, for perfect morality is the indispensable foundation of the holy life. Flashes of insight may come at various times, but full enlightenment is impossible without perfect purity. Hence, in his feeling, speech, thought and deed, the *bhikkhu* abstains from harming any living creature; from taking what is not freely given; from lying, slanderous, malicious, idle and rude speech; from intoxicants; from all sensual indulgences.

Gradually, he attains 'success in moral habit', as the Buddha says. With success in moral habit, one of the greatest steps towards freedom from *dukkha* and slavery to the Lord of Death has been taken. This step makes possible the next one, namely, success in concentration. For when the heart is pure the mind remains undistracted by any stimulus. When the mind is calm and poised, concentration is easy. Poised concentration is a creative state in which the mind sees with nice discernment the lucid truth, untarnished and undistorted by the falsifications and misinterpretations which are the inevitable consequences of the influence of the impure heart. Whenever morality is weak, perception is clouded. Thereupon, mental concentration bears ill-fruit, driving one to wrong-doing.

What are some of the implications of success in concentration?

First, attention can be easily centred in the subjects of meditation. Buddhaghosa enumerates forty such subjects in his *Visuddhimagga* (Path of Purification). Various religious disciplines have their own subjects. All these are effective in bringing about that transformation of the individual mind, and particularly of the mode of awareness from moment to moment, which is the fruit of the *brahma*-faring. The *saṃsāric* or worldly mind, aware of everything in the mode of mortality, is transformed into the pure mind, the *vohu-mano* or good mind as Zarathushtra taught, which is aware in the mode of the Deathless. Herein, the mind is empty of greed, void of hate and free of delusion. Hence, in contrast to superficial knowledge, which confuses by its diversifications, there is *whole* knowledge, unstained by attachment or aversion. And the lustful possessiveness which masquerades as love becomes transformed and matured into the truly compassionate heart. Such a mind has the strength to remain turned away from all worldliness, wide awake to the ephemeral character of the existential world. It is pre-eminently this type of mind which knows how to deal with everyday affairs and problems.

Another important implication of success in concentration is the capacity to remain constantly mindful. There is the moving, and there is the unmoving. The silent watcher within oneself observes the moving, which is the mortal becoming-process, without clinging to it and without attempting to reject it. To use theistic parlance, the hand of God sweeps round the sphere of eternal being, and point-events, or space-time-conditionality, are manifest. This is the moving. In the Hindu context, the sphere of eternal being is *ākāśa*, which is simultaneously the limitless void and the conditioned fullness, unmoving. Brahman, or Very God of Very God, is the Transcendent. Mind, in its original natural state, is the unmoving; in its *saṃsāric*, mortal state, the state of sin and *dukkha*, it is the moving. The self-conscious individual here in the world, who constitutionally possesses the ability to watch silently, can exercise constant mindfulness of the moving, or he can remain concentratedly attentive in the unmoving. During mindfulness of the moving, no fresh bonds confining one to *dukkha* are forged. The turbid torrent of the world's evil froths past, leaving one unsullied. By concentrated attentiveness in the unmoving, the world-stream is cleansed, and mankind is healed and carried on the honey-sweet current of divine life towards Nirvana. This is spiritual healing. This *bodhisattvic* activity of concentrated attentiveness in the unmoving is transcendent karma (action), without which, starved of love, wisdom and grace, no longer upheld by the eternal *Dharma*, the worlds would fall into ruin.

A major consequence of success in concentration is the transmutation of all the past *saṃsāric* karma. There are two main aspects to this. The first concerns the earlier stage. Here, in the practice of mindfulness, one traces the uprising desire or thought or feeling, or dream, or situation or action, to its precedent causes or to its predetermining conditions in the past. Each such cause, or complex of conditions, which is a mental impression stored in the subconscious mind, a *vāsana*, is observed fully. It is seen emerging out of one's own *avidyā* (ignorance), and one's own *taṇhā* (thirst for sentient existence). It is seen that all forms of sentient existence, painful or pleasurable, bad or good, are all subject to death, are all *dukkha*, are not *attā*. If seen fully, there is an end to that karma and to the production of future similar karma. Thus there is a healing of that malady of the mind. This is perfect psychotherapy, in which both the disease and also its roots, namely delusion and egoism, greed and hate, are all 'stopped without remainder', to use the Buddha's phrase. He who succeeds in this ceases to react helplessly to any stimulus. Instead, he is able to make a right, deliberate response. And far more important, he is freed of all fantasies in his waking state. The ills of the past are transformed into virtues and powers by the alchemy of mindfulness, *sammā sati*.

Not all the *vāsanas*, the vast hordes of impressions of the incalculable past, can be worked out in this manner. There is a heap left over, like a loose mountain of dry grass. Now, each time one concentrates attention upon a deep spiritual reality, such as the teacher, the gods, the Elohim, the Ameshaspands, the values which are spiritual powers, the Supreme Being, Brahman, the Tathāgata, the Dharmakāya, the Holy Church which is the Body of Christ; each time one pronounces the Holy Name or a sacred *mantra*, well understanding its meaning and its potency; each time one enters upon and abides in the deep states of consciousness, the *jhānas*, the divine communion, *sammā samādhi*—each time one does any of these, a psycho-spiritual fire flames up, like Moses' God in the burning bush, and a myriad sins of the past—for that is what these clinging mental impressions are—are all burnt up and transmuted into the primordial mind-stuff of the world. This supreme purification occurs in the later, more advanced stages, and particularly in those *dhamma* which are more excellent than knowledge and vision. He who has been thus purified is free of the tyranny of dreams in his sleep.

The root of attaining knowledge and vision is right investigation, which includes enquiry into the truth about ourselves. First, the preceptor or the guru tells one what is fit to be told to the beginner. This is *śravaṇa,* or the hearing stage. The next is *manaṇa* which is reflection upon what is heard. Logical reasoning is hard at work here, and its fruit is the right and lucid guiding idea which forms the subject of that concentrated attention which is *nididhyāsana,* the third stage, which culminates in *sammā samādhi.* What is the knowledge and vision one wins thereby? The scriptures tell us much of this. Also, many questions, such as *What am I?, Where do I come from?, Where am I going?, By what path do I arrive at the haven, the saranaṃ?* are all answered. The Buddha unequivocally affirmed the Transcendent, which is both the source and the goal. The Unborn, the Unmade, is our source, in which we start in the darkness of ignorance. Our goal is Nirvana. Our *brahmacarīya,* the moving in Brahman, the walking in God as theistic mystics say, restores us to the Unborn, the Unmade. But this restoration is a reinstatement as Tathāgata, whereby the Unborn, the Unmade, is now Nirvana. The darkness of ignorance is in fact transmuted into the never-setting, never-rising but perpetually shining sun of Enlightenment.

Something like this is the vision. The essence of the knowledge we gain, the pith, is first that our existential human-ness is *dukkha,* originated and sustained by the twelve *nidānas,* of which ignorance and the thirst for sentient existence are the chief; and next that freedom from ignorance and the thirst for sentient existence, by treading the Way, spells the end of *dukkha,* or the realization of Nirvana.

The possession of knowledge and vision is associated with conditioned deliverance. There is, however, something more excellent, by which one realizes the emancipation that is unconditioned. And the Buddha expounds this as the entry into successively profounder ecstatic states, the *jhānas* and *samāpattis*, culminating in the unconditioned Nirvana. The abiding in these deep states of consciousness is the very core of the religious experience. Let there be no misconception or equivocation whatsoever about this. The very heart of religious discipline is the utter purification of body and soul; and this is the indispensable foundation for the religious experience, whose grades culminate in the supreme realization of the Transcendent, namely, Nirvana, *here-now*.

Let us briefly consider the landmarks of these ecstatic states. They begin with the pacifying of sense-conscious activity. Thus the mind becomes harmoniously co-ordinated, its energies self-contained or continent. Now one experiences the strength and joy of peaceful contemplation. Next, the discursive activity of the mind comes to rest. Now the various forms of sense-consciousness are quite pacified, and so the mind becomes unified—the *ekāgratā* stage—in which the whole mind comes into its own for the first time. But although the speech-thought process which is the result of sense-impressions ceases, and the intensity of calm and dispassion begins to supervene, the deep significance of words representing keynotes of the interior spiritual life is still operative. In the *Anupada Sutta*, the Buddha, speaking of Sāriputta in meditation, details these as feeling, perception, will, thought, desire, determination, etc. Devotees and mystics have talked of divine love, God's consolations, faith, goodness, truth, etc.

The fourth *jhāna* is an important landmark. There is complete equanimity here. The operation of karmic law can be seen in its fullness, as well as the true meaning of rebirth. The transcending of the limited functioning of consciousness in terms of the finite can take place in this fourth *jhāna* by the cessation of all sensory perception and form consciousness. This means that transcending the mortal, the *jhāni* now not only has the vision of the immortal but actually experiences the deathless consciousness. He passes into the state of the realization of infinity; of the infinity of *ākāśa*, the source stuff of manifestation, and of *viññāṇa*, the cognizing consciousness which perceives every manifestation. (Think of infinity as beginninglessness and endlessness, and not in terms of size.) Here at last he has taken a major step in putting an end to the state of *dukkha*, of the far from the infinite. Time, sensation and death are over. This indeed is good cheer.

Assured of the deathless, he enters the plane of no-thing. One might imagine that in realizing infinity, the plane of no-thing was included. No so. The *jhāni* has a psycho-physical organism. No matter how purified, refined or etherealized, it is still the concrete expression, amongst other things, of the subtlest, the most spiritual elements that the individual discriminative consciousness, the *viññāṇa*, can perceive or feel. But in that excellent abiding in no-thing, like a winged horse pulling up all his tethers, the *jhāni* experiences the dissolution of the subtlest and profoundest archetypal ideas, or *saṃkhāras*, built in during uncounted ages. And the names of these *saṃkhāras* are God and Iśvara, *ātman* and *brahman*, Nirvana and the kingdom of heaven, eternity and time, the void and the plenum, death and perfection and immortality, and so on. The dark night of the soul when God forsakes the devotee is repeated here at a transcendental level. Here indeed the voidness, the *śūnyatā*, is truly realized, and also, paradoxically enough, the *pūrnam*, the fullness. Hence, the complete interdiffusion of inter-related particulars, and of the whole and the particular, is also realized. This is the end of sin. This is where the evil one, Māra, cannot find the *jhāni* who has gone beyond the edge of the world. But with this final dissolution of all the *saṃkhāras*, it seems as if the dissolution or disappearance of the *viññāṇa* itself takes place. The last vestige of separate self is gone, and selflessness is realized through the no-thing awareness.

It is not surprising, therefore, that with this tracklessness of the *viññāṇa*, neither-perception-nor-non-perception and the stopping of all perception and feeling complete the list of those *dhamma* which are more excellent than knowledge and vision. The words perception and feeling are used in a transcendental sense in this context. But note carefully that after declaring that the stopping of feeling and perception, which is Nirvana, is the most excellent abiding, the Buddha says: 'And having seen by *paññā*, his *āsavas* are utterly destroyed.' Let us try to see more clearly what this means.

The Buddha calls each of the deep modes of consciousness a *dhamma*, and each such *dhamma* is more excellent than knowledge and vision. The Sanskrit word *dharma* is derived from the root *dhri*, meaning to uphold. What is it that is upheld? Way back in the *Rig Veda* it is taught that the great gods, Agni, Varuna, Indra, Soma and all the others, uphold *ritam*, the eternal law and order, spiritual and moral. This *ritam* is good and perfect. Whatsoever a man does, diligently following the way of the gods, is *dharma*, the upholding of *ritam*. The *dharma* which leads man to Nirvana is an upholding of *ritam*. This is religion and religious practice. Each step of the deep abidings, which the Buddha designates as a *dhamma*, is a religious teaching and a practice resulting in a mode of awareness, and these different modes range up to Nirvana.

Paññā is unerring insight. What is it that is seen by *paññā*? In the transcendent awareness of true superconciousness, the supreme truth is seen, which means that the supreme truth is experienced. For in this transcendent sphere, the seer, the seen and the seeing have become one, have become supreme being which is also consciousness and bliss—*sadchid ānanda*. In this being-consciousness-bliss, inconceivable through the ordinary functioning of our mind, is subsumed our *viññāṇa*, which in the earlier *samapātti* had become self-less, had become trans-personal. So the Buddha teaches that the Tathāgata is trackless; we will not find his *viññāṇa*, and whatever we say about it in the context of existentiality is absurd. So, too, the great *jīvanmuktas*, the perfected holy ones of Upanishadic lore, declared that they had realized the *ātman*, had become *brahman*. This transcendent realization, the supreme religious experience possible to man, is the uttermost freedom from *saṃsāric* existence and awareness. This, the realization of the *ātman*, is supreme truth. Through *paññā* is seen this truth. Through *paññā*, the dark force that clouds the eternal light and gives birth to separate *viññāṇa* is seen and fully understood. Through *paññā* is won the ability henceforth to maintain and manifest the transcendent glory of the immortal in each and every grade of conscious existence here on returning from the realization of Nirvana to our blessed, ever-sustaining, silently-enduring Mother Earth. For ever and ever, *avidyā* and *taṇhā,* sin and suffering and death are gone. The world is overcome—no, not overcome, but by immortal love transformed into the similitude of eternal beauty.

Therefore the Buddha taught that, having seen by *paññā,* his *āsavas* are utterly destroyed. *Āsava* means an outflow or exudation in the sense of something wrong, of a malaise. In the context of religion, an outflow of what into what? It is the outflow of consciousness into the forms of lust, into clinging to worldly existence, into speculative views, into states of illusion and delusion. Such exudations are cankers. But in the final consummation, having seen by *paññā,* having become *dhamma* and become *brahman,* one's consciousness does not outflow, like a running sore, into *dukkha.* The possibility of such an exudation is rooted out by the *jhāni* who has successfully gone *all* the way.

When the perfected holy one returns from the excellent abidings to the ordinary everyday consciousness, his mind stands poised, utterly pure and free. Unshakable freedom of mind is his.

Mindfulness and the Fourth Precept

(1966)

DESIRE AND EGO, ignorance and lack of discipline, make up a vicious complex. Desire is blind and amoral in its primitive upsurge; its domain is the sphere of duality. The ego-sense is an expression of the misperception of true being, which is ego-less being. A part of true being is regarded as a permanent entity and continual efforts are made to constrain life to revolve round this centre. He who is quite free of egocentricity is one who has reached his true home.

Blind desire and egocentricity are associated with ignorance. The very nature of the organism strengthens the desire for pleasurable sensation; it also gives rise to painful experience, to disappointment and suffering. When the conflict of pleasure and suffering impels a man to seek the resolution of this conflict from within himself, then begins the transformation of ignorance into wisdom.

Mindfulness effects this transformation. Repentance, the turning away from worldliness, is hardly possible without seeing that from which one must turn away. Therefore observe action and speech and the flow of thought and feeling from moment to moment. Continuous watchfulness, impossible in the early stages, becomes an established awakened condition even when asleep (see *Majjhima Nikāya*, I. 249) through constant practice.

One must be a fully observant witness, without censure or approval, without aversion or attraction. Censure can give rise to a guilt complex with all its undesirable concomitants; approval, on the other hand, can lead to pride and complacency. Neither guilt nor pride are conducive to freedom from the ego-sense. Nor are aversion or attraction, each of which indicates that that which is observed is master of the observer. Censure, approval, aversion and attraction all prevent calm and freedom, vision and insight.

The profound depths of the mind are invested with the peace and harmony which are healing powers of egoless being. Directing calm attention to the surface states of the psyche transforms them. Just as the physical cells of the living body are characterized by the power of self-healing, there is, so to say, a self-righting tendency in the psyche. A physical wound is dressed or a fatigued man rests in order to have a chance for a restoration to health. So too, there is a chance for the restoration of the psyche to holiness when the surface disturbance of the mind is 'treated' by calm observation.

Mindfulness acquaints one with oneself. Great courage is needed in order to persevere with this practice, for the self-revelation invariably shocks one and much emotional and intellectual distress is experienced. When courage fails, energy flags, the enormity of the task crushes one, depression envelops one like a black thundercloud, the terror of the unknown depths of the soul and the fear caused by seeing what one does see even in the early stages overwhelm one, do not cry for help, nor fly to a friend for consolation, nor delve into a book of wisdom. Keep quiet, or else one is sure to get hurt. Simply look. Under the compassionate gaze of the sleepless immortal eyes, the confusion of the mind and the turmoil in the heart come to rest.

When an object, say a lamp in a shop window, is seen, one may make a pure registration: there is a lamp in the shop window. There is no reaction of thought or feeling here. Or one may make a registration accompanied by a judgement and a desire. 'I like it, I want it.' Here it is desire as attraction. 'I don't like it, I shan't have that one.' Here it is desire as aversion. The desire-reaction is a disturbance and serves as a fetter. But neither the sense of sight, *per se,* nor the lamp, *per se,* is a fetter, nor is the objective seeing, *per se*, a disturbance. In the *Samyutta Nikāya* (IV. 281), Chitta, a householder, says:

> Well, sirs, the eye is not a fetter of objects, nor objects a fetter to the eye. But the desire and lust that arise owing to the pair of them, that is the fetter.

Now one can understand why the great religious disciplines of the world so strongly warned the mystic or yogi to beware of the senses. The Buddha constantly talks of the 'peril of the senses' and of 'carefully guarding the senses'. The peril against which one carefully guards oneself is the arising of desire and its accompanying lust, greed, hate, delusion, anxiety and fear, when stimuli from sense objects are registered by the senses. It must always be remembered that religious discipline insists upon the right use of the senses, and the development of the senses to the highest possible pitch purely as trustworthy instruments of observation. Now also one understands why the Buddha declares that he holds aloof or refrains from shows, performances of any sort, the arts, and in short everything that makes up the ordinary life of the world. Whatever it is, it distracts attention from the Transcendent.

Perhaps the most tiresome disturbance in everyday life is constant chatter—inconsequential, useless, misinforming, misleading, mischievous, confusion- and trouble-making, discourteous, unrefined, seductive, loud, blundering, frivolous, slanderous, malicious, evil-designing, lying, devilish chatter. India has an excellent teaching here: if what is to be said is truthful, kind and useful, then say it; but if it is not, then silence is best.

As the witness self comes more into his own, one becomes increasingly sparing of speech. The immense amount of energy economized thereby is used in purer observation and clearer thinking. When the noisy leak of pointless chatter is repaired, the quiet well of understanding fills. Then indeed conversation is a refreshing draught; at times, a healing stream of the waters of life. True conversation is as rare as good poetry. In its place rages that bastard usurper, ceaseless chatter. Save him who has an understanding heart, everyone ceaselessly chatters in one or other of two ways: he speaks aloud for others to hear, or he chatters silently in his own mind. He can shut his mouth, but he is utterly impotent to stop his mental chatter.

What is it all about? Mainly oneself. The word 'I', or the image of oneself, is overwhelmingly predominant; the centre round which the silent chatter is compelled to reel in tipsy fashion. To one who is mindful, day-dreaming (or fantasy life) and dream life are valuable revealers of oneself. Fantasy life is a perfect example of 'being tossed on the stormy ocean of *saṃsāra*'. Each person's existence, as observed, is a manifestation of a conscious living being moving through a series of events. This constitutes each person's *saṃsāra*. The manner in which he is aware at any moment, his state of consciousness, is of prime importance here; the succession of events is of secondary importance.

The state of consciousness which is entangled in the web of events is worldly consciousness. The disentangled consciousness, in pure freedom, is undeludedly aware of the web of events for exactly what it is. It is the liberated consciousness which has realized the Transcendent. The difference is not a difference between *this* world (of the flesh and the devil) and *that* world (of God). There is only one world, one reality. There is only unitary being, a single becoming-process. The difference is that the consciousness which was limited in ignorance, unawakened, has emerged into the freedom of enlightenment, fully awakened.

The ordinary man, dimly glimpsing and feebly aspiring to the divine, and a Buddha who is continuously at home in the Transcendent, equally live in the one world, the whole reality, in which events flow in a continuous stream. That means that the ordinary man and God incarnate are both inside *saṃsāra*. But the one is tossed on the stormy sea, always in peril of death, whereas the other securely walks the waves and can still them by a simple command. The one is mortal, the other is immortal, although the outward form of each, the body, will die at its appointed time and disintegrate.

Fantasy life and dream life are a non-stop cinema show. On the screen is projected the ordinary man's *saṃsāra* or 'worldly' existence. Dream life reveals him with some of the controls off. There is little that can be done about it in the early stages. But fantasy life in the waking state should be watched with the utmost care and in as full detail as possible.

Inherent in every force is the due result of its own activity. One's silent mental life, so securely secret from any mortal's gaze, is wholly open to itself, even if the day-dreaming person himself is only vaguely conscious or even forgetful of it. Being wholly open to itself, it 'metes out due result' to itself, for that is inherent in its very being.

Let us express this in theistic terms. God sees everything. Now if the day-dreamer co-operates with the Divine, by mindful observation, then a potential Son of God is stirring into divine activity; the creative word of God may be brought forth. The senseless chatter of unawakened man, on the other hand, makes confusion—the Tower of Babel? The opening of the inner eye slowly restores order and a cosmos emerges—the integrated personality which is true man. Thereupon speech, which is one of man's profoundest powers, comes into harmony with the Creative Word. When it is in perfect harmony, the full-statured Son of God 'sings for joy' and utters only prophetic speech.

Therefore watch this fantasy play, this ceaseless, silent chatter which is speech diseased. As long as this cancer is not healed, no man obtains even a modicum of knowledge of mind, including his own mind, and of the vast powers of mind. To heal the mind, quiet observation is the essential means.

Such observation immediately shows that fantasy life is disorderly. No restraint is exercised from within. The silent chatter flutters hither and thither, moved by every idle sense stimulus from without or by memory or desire from within. The substance and form of the fantasies reveal one's past conditioning, how far ego and desire have been satisfied or frustrated, what has been repressed, what are one's secret longings or ambitions. They expose the cleavage between the private inner life of feeling and thought on the one hand and the outer life of speech and action on the other. They indicate one's temperament, one's maturity or immaturity. They show whether one's mind is vague and loose-knit or clear and concentrated, what knowledge one has, and what are one's biases, prejudices, preconceptions and assumptions.

Above all, fantasies clearly reveal inward morality. Watch the fantasies of hate and anger—the terrible things one does to the hated one! Watch the fantasies of lust for power, possessions, sex, personal superiority, doing good, becoming perfect, serving God and putting the whole world right! Watch the fantasies of all the subtle forms of indulgence, artistic and intellectual, sporting and exhilarating; and of planning out the lives of one's own children, and of others not so close!

Mindfulness will show how desire and ego are the source of this fantastic dissipation through mental chatter of what should be a wealth of soul-strength, of virtue. And if there is steady perseverance in mindfulness, without censure or approval, aversion or attraction, one sees that the heart of inward morality is love and wisdom in active harmony. For all those vices which breed sins against fellow-men, such as ill-will, jealousy, anger and sexual lust, are transformed into love, and all those defects which ease the paths and invite the occasions for wrong-doing, such as stupidity, pig-headedness, conceit, delusion and ignorance, are transformed into wisdom. Only the wise can truly love; only the loving heart can be truly wise.

In time, one understands clearly the consequence to oneself and to others of one's reactions and desires. As this understanding grows, vain pursuits and the harsh misuse of life energy are naturally relinquished. As inward balance, purity, equanimity and wisdom grow, the power of the soul flows out increasingly as love in all its varying forms. And in thought and feeling one observes the moral precepts, and inward morality tallies with outward morality.

Mindfulness has to become a permanent state, effortlessly maintained. There is no end to the growth of virtue. The moment one's soul-strength remains undirected, the tendency to lapse presents a grave danger. This is so all along the Way whilst one is living in the body. For this psycho-physical organism lives not transcendentally in a dimension of perfect freedom which is perfect harmony with divine law, but in a system where relativity, dualism and reciprocity prevail. Consider, for example, that fifteen billion cells composing the physical body clamour for self-reproduction. Their combined cacophony helps to slope one into unpremeditated or inappropriate sexual activity if watchfulness slackens off for a moment. Many are the romantic failures—temporary only, of course!—in the annals of religion and mysticism and yoga the world over, when alluring *apsarā** and nodding neophyte were in close proximity; or when a sudden reversal of judgment in a moment of forgetfulness precipitated one into the very depth out of which one had climbed in the course of years. Forgetfulness, unmindfulness, is the most powerful ally of the devil.

Mindfulness is the instrument of true repentance. There are those temperaments which recoil from the teaching that by arduous, passive watchfulness man realizes sinlessness. They think in terms of the contrite heart, repentant, turning to God with love and faith, and being washed of sin through divine grace. But man's task is to stay clean, to remain repentant, turned away from evil. What the heart of faith and love can evoke from the divine is stained by the foolish head and the clumsy hand. And so that growing towards that glorified state of 'I and the Father are one' through the grace of the Transcendent, the very immanence of God in man, may be treacherously betrayed by the unmindfulness of man. Foolishness and wrong action cannot be averted without constant mindfulness. The seeker of God needs both the impulsion of devotion and the direction of knowledge.

The major aspect of the purification of the intellect is the discipline by which one wins freedom from all mere beliefs, from all imposed disciplines that have the object of gaining preconceived ends, from all unwarranted assumptions and preconceptions, from all bias and prejudice. For the *religieux*, the 'discipline' of theological, scientific, philosophical and other studies is an acquisition of 'mere knowledge,' often a burden rather than an asset. Purification of the mind rather than acquisition by the mind is indispensable for the realization of the

*Heavenly nymph

Transcendent. Whatever the unpurified mind obtains by acquisition—and in nearly all cases such acquisition is at least partly an indulgence of intellectual greed—always distorts. It stands between man and the truth. The purified mind, free of distortion, is in a continuously creative condition; that is, it sees truly, immediately, and expresses itself spontaneously in action.

Trust springs where a stir of inward awareness, inexplicable in itself, is on the march towards vision. When the richness of experience, conjoined with the loving labour of purification, have taken one to the edge of the dark abyss, the void is illuminated. The inexplicable has become clear, quite simple; childlike trust has blossomed into faith.

The purification of the mind is intimately interlinked with moral development, for morality in thought and feeling cannot come to full flower whilst there is the intellectual disease of bias and prejudice, preconception and assumption. Morality must not stop short at the boundaries of reciprocity, for then it topples under sufficient provocation into the abyss of immorality. Virtue circumscribed is the devil's toy gun. Virtue unbounded is spiritual value.

Mindfulness is the means for effecting this purification. In addition to its being practised without censure or approval, without aversion or attraction, one must also practise it without saying right or wrong. For mindfulness shows up the inadequacies of all that one regarded as right. The present, inadequate right cannot be replaced by an absolute or perfect right, say by being told what it is, if indeed the perfect right can ever be told. What one hears or reads is inwardly grasped only to the extent that one has already achieved that rightness within oneself. *The* right constantly emerges from within as one becomes purer. A fixed standard of judgement would defeat the purpose of this discipline.

Paying complete attention to the whole situation is true mindfulness. For this, it is necessary to be free of all beliefs, of all the burden of the past, of all authorities. For any belief, on however great an authority it be based, is an assumption. Hence one's own mind is unfree. And the unfree mind cannot see truth. Any patient person will see the tremendous implications of this. Whoso aspires, and dares, may realize the immeasurable. There is no authoritative instruction to give or ideal to follow. There is no particular way. Yet, seek out the way—your own way. Every way which is a borrowed or dictated way comes at last to a dead-end. But your own way—and you *are* a self-responsible, unique individual in reality—is the way which allows you continual emergence. Your own way is no other than your own mindfulness. It is the way of everlasting life, of sweet savour, without a moment of taint or stagnation.

Mindfulness will reveal that some of the most serious blocks to this consummation are one's own religious beliefs. Then comes deep distress which strikes one down when cherished beliefs are seen to be illusions, tacit assumptions to be groundless and preconceptions to be unwarranted. Self-confidence and the sense of inward security are rudely shaken. One is most reluctant to relinquish the familiar intellectual and spiritual landscape, terrified to turn one's back upon what seemed safe ground and wing an uncharted flight into the trackless open. And this open seems to be nothing but an all-devouring emptiness, for all the hitherto familiar meaningfulness has completely vanished and there is not a sign in the heavens or in the earth to give even one single indication of any *thing*. There is but the vast blank of no-thing. The wings of the spirit are truly terrible, an invisible fire scorching every resource, a petrifying chill freezing head and heart and hand into immobility.

Now is the moment. Let go of everything—ego, self, God, master, truth, love, values, knowledge, good, evil, everything. Let them go absolutely. Beware of holding on to the slightest reservation, the rotten thread that the faint-hearted stupidly mistake for an anchoring chain.

Now is the moment of the *no-thing*. The whole of ever-dying time is not equal to this moment of poised eternity. It hurts—and you experienced a similar hurt when you were squeezed out of your mother's womb—and it hurts enough to wring out tears from the eyes of the soul. But tears must flow and wash away all vision-obscuring dust.

In this condition of revelation, the heart wholly understands the Unborn, Unbecome, Unmade.

Wisdom and Compassion

(1967)

WE HUMANS POSSESS a body evolved out of the animal kingdom. Its heritage includes the fruits of the conflict embodied in Darwin's notion of 'the survival of the fittest'. All our knowledge about it is material. The spiritual, the transcendent, is the unknown, the infinite. It cannot be brought into the field of the known; it cannot be held in the measure of the finite. By the fading away of this THAT, the immeasurable IS. Then, its eternal light shines unobstructedly through a transparent THIS. By the fading away of all knowledge, wisdom works. We, as creatures who are self-consciously separate, will never know truth. Yet it is the truth alone which transmutes us. Our task is to awaken.

The living body has a pleasure-pain mechanism. The brain receives impulses, pleasurable or painful, and responds accordingly. With more than a million years of development, this brain has grown into an extraordinarily subtle and complex organ. One of its marvellous faculties is memory. Unfortunately for us, the mind, corrupted by the memory of pleasure, becomes the slave of desire. This is the desiring-conceiving mind. Memory makes the mind hark back again and again to the past, which is modified or developed with the assistance of imagination, and again we are hot on the scent of further sensational excitements.

But the past is dead. The resuscitation of the past means that a degenerative habit of mind is formed. So the mind stagnates, becomes dull and stupid, often criminally stupid. 'The mind is the slayer of the Real; let the disciple slay the slayer,' says the *Book of the Golden Precepts*. Looking backward upon the past is complemented by speculative imagining about the future. These backward and forward glances help to build up the illusion of the continuity of a postulated entity or self called 'I', which is supposed to grow, develop, control, direct, purify, reincarnate, tread the path and reach Nirvana, etc.

This postulated entity, the 'I' or the ego, is the one that sometimes says, 'I am not my body or thoughts or emotions, but an integral part and parcel of an immutable, eternal, ultimate reality.' This postulate, found in various religions, is contradicted in Buddhist teachings, but many Buddhists actually behave and live just as the ego-holders do. This illusory 'I' is set up over and against the organism, the temporary, changing pattern in the becoming process. Thus from within ourselves originates the subject-object duality: 'I', the subject, set against my organism, the object—and therein arise a host of conflicts.

The mind is the villain of the piece. So successful is it, that we say of this erotic, errant mind that it is rational, perceptive, wise and compassionate, or that it can become so. But the mind is concerned with self-preservation, with ego-continuity. Therefore it sets up goals and ideals, then lays down plans and devises techniques to fulfil them. Every thought-made, mind-projected ideal or goal is only an ego-projection. Every method or constraining discipline produces an intensification of the self-centre. This self-centre can be concretized into an Almighty God sitting on a throne, or a Brahma breathing out and breathing in vast universes. But all these dear, celestial folk are in trouble, in *dukkha* as the Buddha pointed out in the *Brahmajāla Sutta*.

All the ideas, knowledge, memories, imaginations, anticipations, preoccupations and plannings of the mind have a proper sphere of activity, namely, the mechanical process of everyday material and cultural life. But all the activity of the duality-perpetuating mind blinds our third eye, the eye of wisdom. This conceiving-desiring mind, this chatter-box of which we are so vainly proud, is indeed the slayer of the Real, and, what is so much nearer and meaningful to us, the spoiler of our humanity, the assassin of love.

Now in relation to wisdom, the business of the mind is not to interfere but to observe with complete attentiveness to the totality of life, *here-now*. Wisdom is not a bundle of thoughts or verbal statements concretely embodying formless, mysterious, transcendental things called truths. We cannot search for wisdom, or acquire it. But when we are fully awake to what *is* here and now, namely, our illusions and delusions, pleasure or pain, joy or grief, the room, the event, then we are wise, or, wisdom is unobstructedly active in us. This *mahā-prajñā* is not something we can hold in our fists, for this direct seeing of reality is a 'limb of enlightenment', a no-thing.

Truth, in the religious sense, is the intense white-hot awareness of the living, total what-is as it changes from moment to moment. It is the *śūnyatā-phala-samādhi* of the Buddha. Now, contrast science or worldly knowledge with religious knowledge, *avidyā* or not-seeing with *vidyā* or seeing. Science comes within the realm of thought-experience, of word-things. It proceeds from the known to the unknown. But this unknown is only a hidden known playing hide-and-seek with the accumulated known. It is confined to the realm of the manifest, of mortality. By contrast, unerring insight, *prajñā*, does something quite different. It functions where we do *not* know intellectually, when we are *not* looking for an answer which can be related to the already known. Insight sees into, it understands directly the inexpressible unknown. Insight meets the totally new, the source of creative renewal. Our pattern-forming mind afterwards gives mental interpretation, verbal or pictorial form, to this direct seeing. Thereupon the unknown, the unconditioned reality, is constrained into limited, conditioned form, into mere knowledge. Thus, esoteric wisdom is stepped down, *degraded*, into exoteric teaching, mere knowledge, which is just ignorance.

Consider how the Buddha extolled going forth from the life of the home into the homeless state. Esoterically, might this mean going forth from the limitation of the conditioned familiar into the non-conditioned unfamiliar? Does this not signify such total renunciation of the known that self disappears, and the immortal Transcendent IS *here-now* in all the beauty of its all-loving aloneness?

Let us consider together what we mean by the known, and what we mean by understanding or direct seeing, by *buddhi*. Ordinarily, when the senses function, there is a reaction of *taṇhā*, of desire-thought: an attraction or repulsion, approval or disapproval, a judgement of good or bad, right or wrong. When desire arises, it arises dually. Consciously, there is a straight statement of the desire, a diction. Unconsciously, there is a contra-diction, an urge which says 'I don't want it' or 'I want to be free of the desire.' *Taṇhā* is the very stuff of conflicting duality. Consciously, the desire is given mental shape by the verbalizing process, that is, it is expressed as a thought-form. All our sense observation and all our ordinary thinking is heavily charged with *taṇhā*. This binds. It is *dukkha*. If thought-desire is gratified, further desire is bred. If frustrated, resentment, a more aggressive egoistic will to succeed and an ever more burning desire is bred. Net result—*dukkha*.

To start with, then, all our ordinary knowledge, thoughts, memories, beliefs, ideas, conclusions, aspirations, ideals, goals—everything contained within our mind-box—is poisoned or distorted by *taṇhā*; all of it is related to a self-centre. Thus, when we observe ordinarily, all our observation and what we are pleased to call intellectual understanding, is vitiated from the start, rotten to its very core.

Our ordinary observation and our intellectual understanding are not worth the name of mindfulness or of understanding. This intellectual understanding is the bond-slave of the dead past. It is an automatic repetition-machine, uncreative, unteaching, unhealing. It has its place only in the realm of the conditioned, of *dukkha*. What we often call intuition, understanding by feeling, is similarly vitiated. This feeling is also a mental process, a hidden-thought or non-verbalised process. Like intellectual understanding, it is under the sway of desire. It is of the dead past, or shall we say of the dying passing, of the conditioned, of *dukkha*. The apparent movement or progress by the activity of this kind of intuitive and/or intellectual understanding is only a modification of the *saṃsāric* pattern, only another bed of nails. It is not enlightenment, not freedom.

To escape out of this *saṃsāric* hell-fire, a path was proclaimed by the Buddha, just as other great teachers proclaimed other paths to salvation. In the Noble Eightfold Path, if and when there is *sammā sati*, perfect mindfulness, and *sammā samādhi*, perfect communion in which the total mind is silent, the unconditioned understanding which is unerring insight, *buddhi*, omniscience, comes alive. This is the seeing of the enlightened one, his vision, his *sammā-ditthi*. This is the plenum flashing throughout the void as light. In his first sermon the Buddha repeatedly affirms, 'Then Light arose, Vision arose,' for he has seen through all appearances, and his self, Siddhattha Gotama, transfigured, has dissolved into the transparent reality.

But now, before you begin to sprint along on the path with redoubled energy, eager to enter Nirvana with a bound, or, to acquire a jack-pot of merit as a consolation prize, listen to the *Prajñā-pāramitā*.* Subhuti is questioning the Lord: 'O Lord, is enlightenment attained through an unproduced *dharma*?' 'No, Subhuti.' 'Is then enlightenment attained through a produced *dharma*?' 'No, Subhuti.' 'Is then enlightenment attained neither through a produced nor through an unproduced *dharma*?' 'No, Subhuti.' 'How then is enlightenment attained?' 'Enlightenment is attained neither through a path, nor through a no-path. Just the path is enlightenment, just enlightenment is the path.'

Consider, with love, for love makes wise. What quality distinguishes the teachings of all the great teachers? Is it not the utter originality of the presentation of truth? And remember that originality is not the logical or inevitable consequence of following known paths. This originality in the religious context is quite different from a thinker's thoughts, however original they may be. Thoughts are like inanimate things, at best only *saṃsārically* inspiring, splashing in the mud of *dukkha*. Contrasting with thoughts, which are merely congealed mental patterns, the presentation of the truth is the living word of the holy one, and this word, his speech, is prophecy.

*See *Selected Sayings from the perfection of Wisdom*, tr. E. Conze, London, 1955, p. 115.

It is like this. If I present you today with a frying pan as a token of my affection for you, you will use it again and again to make an egg and tomato dish for me each time I come visiting you. Same old saucepan for dishing me up a meal! Such is the thought of the thinker, a repetitious dishing-up. But if I hold you to my heart and kiss you with pure love, that kiss cannot be stored up, to be used again. There is a new kiss for the new day. The old has completely gone — not lost, but become part of you with a deathlessness that is trackless. Such is the word of the holy one.

You will say: 'But the words of the holy ones *have* been stored up for thousands of years, and *are* repeated, and *are* used again and again.' Yes, unhappily, the words of the holy ones are so used — as mere words. But I am talking about the prophetic word, the Logos, which is the divine conceiving, the Unlimited Transcendence in the holy mind before it is fossilized as a series of linguistic sounds.

The holy one himself is the path, a pure path. We ourselves are also paths; muddy, stony paths. The prophetic word of the holy one is a finger of living light illumining the path, the invisible truth. Our minds lay down the bricks of our thoughts and ideas, and cement them with the rigidities of our uncompassionate ignorance. We lay down paths: not so, the trackless Tathāgatas.

We talk about different paths to perfection meeting at the summit. But, do these paths go up a mountain to a summit; or do they, once formulated, simply go round and round? What, perchance, is the significance of the *bhikkhus'* processional path encircling the great *Stūpa* at Sanchi? There is no pathway *up* to its crowning umbrella, 54 feet above the ground, which stands inviolate. Is not a summit only touched by him who breaks free? Did not Gotama break free of his home? Did not all the holy ones break free of all their bonds, without misdirected violence, but simply by direct seeing? Surely, the summit is *here-now*, not at the end of a path, for all ends are dead-ends. The *here-now* is eternal being — that being universal, rhythmic pulsating which is *sassāṛically* experienced as alternating birth-death. Surely, the summit means the highest intensity of awareness; it means being fully awake.

When there is enlightenment, then the new, the unknown, is present. This unknown is, in Milton's words, 'the radiant shrine, dark with excessive bright', for you the person are no more. The transformed you, Avalokita on high as the *Prajñāpāramitā* has it, sees directly that the form is void and the void is form. You see that the path is no path, Nirvana is *saṃsāra*, and appearance is reality. For you are free of thought-coverings. Like all objects which are intruders in space, all thoughts are intruders in universal mind, all states of consciousness are intruders in pure Attention.

How significant are Mañjuśri's words to Śāriputra in the *Prajñāpāramitā*: 'Enlightenment is not discerned by anyone, nor is it fully known, nor seen, nor heard, nor remembered. It is neither produced nor stopped, neither described, nor expounded. In so far as there is any enlightenment, O Śāriputra, that enlightenment is neither existence nor non-existence. For there is nothing that could be known by enlightenment, nor does enlightenment fully know enlightenment.' Śāriputra asks: 'Has the Lord, then, not fully known the realm of *dharma*?' And Mañjusri answers: 'The Lord has not fully known the realm of *dharma*. For the realm of *dharma* is just the Lord. O Śāriputra, if the realm of *dharma* were something that had been fully known by the Lord, then the realm of non-production could be stopped. But the realm of *dharma* is just the same as enlightenment, for the realm of *dharma* is devoid of existence. "Non-existent are all *dharmas*," that is a synonym of enlightenment, and it is thus that the realm of *dharma* comes to be called thus. For, as the domain of the Buddha, all *dharmas* are non-separateness.'

How shall we see directly, without the darkening interposition of our ideas and beliefs, and the suffocating smoke of our desires and delusions? How shall we fulfil the Buddha's 'In the seeing, only the seen; in the hearing, only the heard;' etc.? First remember there is *no-thing* to see, *no-sound* to hear. Wisdom begins with purified senses. Let us be wholly mindful of the entire, changing situation—see, hear, touch, etc.—without any attachment or aversion, approval or condemnation. Do this without letting recognition—*re*-cognition—of what is being seen or heard, felt or thought, interfere with the mindfulness. This is extremely arduous. But if we do this, we are free of the clutter of the dead past. Our mind is now spacious. It is free, and so it observes anew, as if for the first time; it observes without any conflicts whatsoever, because we are not taking sides, choosing this as against that with respect to all that is observed. When we observe thus, our seeing and hearing and feeling will be full of dancing delight, the sheer joy of the pure activity of the senses, free of *taṇhā*, free of karmic debt, free of illusions. We must not exclude anything from our observation nor make frantic efforts to include everything, for both exclusive concentration and grasping concentration set up conflicts. We must be fully sensitive to everything, observe effortlessly, and live *by* letting live.

You may say: 'But if I merely look and retain nothing, extract no essence, disregard all the past as you suggest, I shall simply be empty-headed. What good is that?'

What-headed are we now? When we observe purely, with full attention, we are experiencing at our most intense. This experiencing gives us self-knowledge; that is, knowledge of the ways of the self. With pure observation there is full understanding of what is observed. The vision is direct, the understanding is perfect, because there is experiencing at its intensest. Therefore the experience, which is the form given by memory, after the event, to experiencing, dissolves away. And also, most important of all, the self-conscious experiencer, that blockhead the 'I', is no more.

Understanding comes not by authority. The sweet bud of understanding is nipped by the cruel frost of authority. Understanding comes not in course of psychological time. Understanding flashes in the still interval between two awarenesses, in the total silence of the mind which is calmly spacious. This silence is timeless, quite beyond psychological time, for psychological time is the conflict of desire's contradictions: of choosing this against that. This silence is not engineered. It is the soundless tone, the rhythmic pulse of Nature's being whose eternity transcends all duration. In this silence, the mind does not decay. It is free of decrepitude through time and deadly death. The body moves on into death the consummator, for the body comes within the orbit of chronological time, which lays desolate the universe. The Buddha dies aged 80. But 80-year-old Siddhattha Gotama dies an ageless, undying Buddha, the ever virgin youth.

With the silence of the mind and the flowering of understanding, you cease to do evil and you cease to pursue good. For you who have gone thus, like Avalokita on high, clearly see that if you resist a thought or feeling out of condemnation, or if you are attracted through approving choice, you will never understand it. But if you observe it unresistingly and follow it to its very end without indulging it in any way, you will have unerring insight into it together with full compassion—*mahāprajñā* and *mahākarunā*.

And this *mahākarunā*, this love grown wise through infinite pity for each and every one in suffering, compels you, the truth-finder, to answer the distress call of your fellow man. And so you speak the word. Your communication *has* to use thoughts, conceptual patterns, words. So there is a stepping down of truth—a sin. Loving too well, you sin. But love must sin thus, although the penalty is death. Yet the wise one, knowing that death is love's redeeming power, sins wisely, and endures a wise, knowing death. Is not the myth that the Buddha-to be, the Bodhisattva, comes down from the Tushita Heaven into the womb of his mother, Mahā-Māyā, a name which means 'the Great Illusion', intended perhaps to teach us love's redeeming power by means of a wise, knowing (that is, deliberate) death?

With the stepping down of the truth, for some a God, for some a Dharma, comes into formal being. A path to salvation is laid down, an interminable treadmill with a hope and a promise and a reward and an attainment at the end of it. Oh, the futility and the misery of it all! But this Valhalla of the gods, built for the ones fattening through the self-becoming ego-expanding process, built by backward giants slavishly toiling for the wretched fruits of lust and power, is doomed to fiery destruction when at last transcendent love indraws a projected ego-self into its own ego-less, thing-less and thought-less eternity.

Because of *mahā-karunā*, it is said that the Bodhisattva vows not to enter Nirvana till all beings have entered, and some say till every blade of grass has reached its salvation.

This is senseless, if taken literally in the worldly context of chronological time and the self-becoming process. Let us try to understand. 'You', a self, never enter 'Nirvana', a state. But because of your *sammā-sati*, this opaque stuff which is the 'you', is now wholly transparent to Nirvana, which always remains unknown by mind-consciousness. Now perhaps we can see that when you enter Nirvana, all beings also enter Nirvana. You, having undergone a transmutation, have entered a new dimension of being, and consciousness is made available for all mankind. Or we may say that when Nirvana touches you, Nirvana touches every being. Only, you are sensitive to the touch, for you are awake; the others, insensitive, shrug it off. We can also see that because all beings have not, on their own, entered Nirvana, you are said to stay out of Nirvana, for you are the compassionate one.

The great compassion wells out when, without false self-identifications with things and people, your mindfulness makes you disappear—one of the psychic powers the holy one has. What might this mean?

One summer day in 1963, I was sitting at ease in the garden, effortlessly paying attention. The birds sang of the joy of creation, not knowing nor caring that death lurked round the corner. Flies settled on dung and perhaps carried disease, but the bright gold sun shone in their wings and green bodies and flashed heavenly light into my soul. And I knew that Sūrya and Agni and all the Vedic gods, and Zeus and Apollo and all the Olympians, and the Elohim and whatever creative agencies there are, 'made' the dung and the fly, and the flower and the ox, and you and me. And I knew we are not just the issue of fertilized ova: we are the heirs of the gods, the divine powers of the Supreme Mystery whence proceeds This-all, this infinite variety of forms veiling the Mystery. Also I saw that we, the ephemeral forms of a moment, a year, a lifetime or of an aeonian world-age—are just the swift-moving ever-born ever-dying flickers of energy-transformations and changes of pressure and temperature; of form and feeling, word and thought; of hunger and thirst, decay and death; of pain and pleasure, grief and joy and storm and peace. And we know moments too deep for speech or act: and then we love the flower and the beast and the earth, and man and devil and God; and imagine we see the beginning and the end of the world, and our fate, and the ineluctable will that sweeps us to an unimagined goal; and sometimes fancy we have met salvation by grace, or received enlightenment in beatitude.

But they—Varuna and Indra and the powers before the throne that made this-all—They said: 'It is we, the sovran lords, who fulfil the behests of the Nameless One through all that is felt and known by you. Your sorrows and successes and confusions and consummations are but the puny expressions of *us*, the great universal powers that play out your little dramas on the world-stage.'

And I knew that this was true. Yet, I also knew that they, the sovran lords, had but a wistful knowledge of my certainty. For my certainty came not only from outside, grew not only from within. It was there before the world was, hidden in the night of sleep till the dawn of awakening. And that golden daybreak glowed with sweet and silent laughter when the still mind spoke its wordless message promising redemption to the powers that toil without Sabbath, making, preserving and moving this vast world, redemption through one man's enlightenment through wisdom, peace through compassion, freedom through that beauty in which self is non-existent. Thus it is that 'you' disappear.

And so, with the unity of life un-marred, the fountains of compassion flow free. You cannot develop compassion; you cannot acquire *mahā-karunā*. But you *can* pay attention, every fleeting moment, to the total changing present. Follow your every thought and feeling without resisting it, till it comes to the end. This is the end of all karma, all sorrow, along that line. Follow the movement of your failure, your sorrow, your fear, so that you reach utter loneliness. Don't move. Stay with that loneliness, one of the last refuges of separate self, pay attention only, do nothing till its very end. Your self-heart will then be transmuted into *the heart*, the heart which is love. But you will first know the reality of death. Let death be. He is your agent of transmutation. And if you just let death be, he will restore you to eternal union with life abundant; and the flow of this life is the stream of compassion. If you let death be, wholly attentive to him, all *dukkha* is transmuted and the immeasurable void is present. Your loneliness is extinguished for ever and you are henceforth the Alone.

By virtue of this *mahā-karunā*, this love which undergoes continuous healing death through your complete attention to the all-this, you will release *mahā-muditā*. You will see the original face of all things and all creatures and all people. You will see them all transfigured, for you will have the blessedness of seeing eternal beauty smiling through the million faces that she shows, the million garbs that she wears for your eternal delight. And your heart will be alight with *mahā-muditā*, transcendent joy. Your silent stillness, *upekkhā*, will be the throbbing heart of love ever renewing the eager pulse of life. For life is perpetual movement, transcendent action. It never arrives. It never reaches a fixed goal, for the fixed goal is a stagnant end-point, irreconcilable with life which is eternally creative. Its moving finger writes on the margins of the eternal mind and laughingly erases the old word as it writes the new. The eternal mind itself is ever empty, spacious, silent.

May each and every one of us be *The Alone*, like a star in the silent solitude of the infinite.

The Open and the Hidden

(1970)

GATHERING a few *siṃsapā* leaves, the Buddha told his *bhikkhus* that, of all the things he had found out, those which he had not revealed were as many as the leaves overhead, whilst those he had revealed were as few as the leaves in his hand. And he explained that he had not revealed whatever was not conducive to living the holy life, but that he had revealed what was conducive to holy living, to perfect wisdom, to Nirvana, namely the Four Noble Truths.

With regard to the *Dhamma* which he had revealed, he declared that he kept nothing back, making no distinction between the exoteric and the esoteric. Doubtless the Enlightened One made his entire teaching clear, during the forty-five years of his ministry, to whoever sat at his feet. But more than two centuries passed before the written records of his teaching began to appear. Do these records contain all that he taught? And exactly as he taught? Do some of them present only essential points in brief, omitting explanatory material? Have no alterations crept in through editing, through interpretations and interpolations by other minds with the passing of the centuries? Furthermore, even assuming that the records contain the Buddha's own words, does your mind or my mind faultlessly grasp their meaning as it was in his mind?

Take one example of a brief presentation omitting explanatory material. In the *Sāmaññaphala Sutta* (D.1.77/8), the Buddha tells King Ajātasattu, and in the *Mahāsakuludāyi Sutta* (M.2.18) he tells Udāyin, that a course has been pointed out, practising which, the learners experience various forms of psychic power, such as diving into the earth, walking on water, flying through the air, and even rubbing the sun and moon with their hands. The 37-page long explanation of this in the twelfth chapter of the *Visuddhimagga* of Buddhaghosa, who flourished nine centuries after the death of the Buddha, seems in parts to be plain and open, whilst other parts stretch credibility to the limit and beyond. None of it, however, will enable me to rub the sun with my hands! Despite the apparent openness of the text, there is present the element of the hidden. If the text is to be read symbolically, then too there is the element of the esoteric.

In the *Mahānidāna Sutta* (D.2.56, 62/3), the Buddha explains to Ananda that mind and body, *nāma-rūpa*, and consciousness, *viññāṇa*, are interdependent. In the *Sāmaññaphala Sutta* (D.1.176), the Buddha tells King Ajātasattu that consciousness is bound up with, and depends upon, the body. It would seem then that with the dissolution of the body, mind and consciousness would also disappear. This sounds annihilationist. Again, when one of the *bhikkhus*, Sāti by name, says that consciousness, like a permanent entity, fares on through births and deaths, the Buddha emphatically refutes this false representation of his teaching, in one of his most earnest discourses, the *Mahātaṇhāsaṇkhaya Sutta* (M.1.256 ff.). Again it would seem that in refuting the eternalist view, the annihilationist view is expressed. But in the *Alagaddūpama Sutta* (M.1.140), the Buddha categorically repudiates the annihilationist view and firmly declares that he does not lay down the cutting off or destruction of the existent entity, the living being, *sato sattassa*. What exactly is implied in this term *sato sattassa*? The words in the text are open, but the meaning is not so open.

Let us now consider another matter. What do we mean by a point? When we put a pencil mark on a piece of paper and say, 'There is a point,' it is actually a blob, not a point. The strict definition of a point tells us that it has no dimensions, neither length nor breadth nor depth. Hence in truth a point is invisible and imponderable. In fact, unlike a blob, which is a thing, a point is no-thing. It is purely a mental construct. It is immeasurable, unconditioned, non-finite.

Mathematically, move this point any distance and we have a line; that is, a length, which is one-dimensional. Move this line in any direction except in its own direction and we have a surface; that is, length and breadth, which is two-dimensional. Move this surface in any direction except in its own plane and we have a three-dimensional form; that is length, breadth and depth. Now the mathematically conceived point, line, surface and form are all invisible physically. The mathematical point and one, two or three dimensions of space can also be mentally conceived separately or together as we please. But if any thing is to be physically seen or handled, its existence needs, simultaneously, all three dimensions of space as well as the dimension of time. Otherwise, no physical body can be perceived by our senses.

So, whilst the Void is the habitat of pure mind, the manifest world of events, energy or things, as apprehended by us through our senses and brain, needs the four-dimensional continuum. All physical substance and all forms of energy, such as electricity, light, heat and so on, have different rates of vibration. Everything manifested is in motion. In ancient India, the primordial substratum of all manifestation was said to be non-moving, in equilibrium. When motion disturbed this equilibrium, different things and phenomena became apparent, having different rates of vibration. Several names were given to this primordial substratum; some called it *prakṛiti*, some *ākāśa*, and so on.

Ākāśa is immeasurable, infinite, inconceivable in any form-sense. It is postulated by some teachers to be the origin of the world as both existence and non-existence, of physical substance and mind-stuff. Like Nirvana, it is in some sense an absolute, for neither *ākāśa* nor Nirvana is born of *kamma*, of cause or of nature (*Milindapañha*, 268). One meaning of *ākāśa* is 'space'. One synonym for *ākāśa* is *śūnya*, the void, possibly comparable to the *inane* of Lucretius in his *De Natura Rerum* (1.330): 'But yet creation's neither crammed nor blocked about by body; there's in things a void.' According to the *Laws of Manu* (1.75–78) and the Sāmkhya and Vedānta systems, the order in which the grosser elements constituting the world are derived from *ākāśa* is as follows: *ākāśa*, air, light or fire, water, earth.

Cicero gives the same order forwards and backwards but omitting light or fire, in his *De Natura Deorum* (2.33). The *Taittirīya Upanishad* (2.1) gives this order: *ātman*, *ākāśa*, air, fire, water, earth, herbs, food, semen, the person. The accounts of *ākāśa* in the Hindu epics are inconsistent with those in the *Purāṇas*. Some say it was created and is perishable, while others say it was not created and is imperishable. Since the world is derived from *ākāśa*, it may be infinite and eternal, or it may not. The Buddha classed these questions among what he called the *indeterminates*, and refused to discuss them as such matters did not conduce to living the holy life, to wisdom, to Nirvana.

It is interesting therefore to note that the Buddha does use the word *ākāśa* in several contexts. For instance, explaining eight causes of earthquakes (*D*.2.107–109), he states the first cause thus: 'This great earth, Ananda, is established on water; water on wind; and the wind rests on *ākāśa*. And at such a time as the mighty winds blow, the waters are shaken by the mighty winds . . . and by the moving water the mighty earth is shaken.' There are several parallels to this in European writers (Windisch, *Mara und Buddha*, 61). Did the Buddha mean his explanation to be taken literally? If so, we today naturally question whether *every* word of the Buddha is incontrovertible truth.

But let us look at some of the other causes of earthquakes which he enunciates. An earthquake occurs when the Bodhisattva consciously and deliberately leaves the Tuṣita Heaven (the heaven of pleasure) and descends into his mother's womb, and when he quits this womb; when the Tathāgata arrives at the supreme and perfect enlightenment, and when he starts the *Dhamma*-wheel rolling; when he consciously and deliberately rejects the remainder of his life, and when he passes entirely away in that utter passing away in which nothing whatever is left behind. In relation to this last cause, are we not reminded of the earthquake and the darkness that fell on the earth and the rending of the veil of the temple at the crucifixion of Jesus?

Do you think we can take all this literally? Did the Buddha speak openly, or is there a hidden meaning?

Let us try a different approach. Siddhattha Gotama, the seeker of perfect wisdom, of Nirvana, is the Bodhisattva whose ordinary life as the heir-apparent in the palace is one of comfort and pleasure—his Tuṣita Heaven. He looks into his own mind. 'The mind is the slayer of the Real,' says the *Book of the Golden Precepts*. It is the prolific womb of illusions. This womb, spoken of as *Hiranyagarbha*, the Golden Womb, is represented as a Supreme God in the *Rig Veda* (10.121), and as a type of consciousness in the *Paingala Upanishad* (1.5). The Bodhisattva deliberately and consciously turns away from the Tuṣita Heaven of pleasure and enters the womb of his mother, Mahā-Māyā—and *mahā-māyā* means the 'great illusion'! Thereupon the 'earth' shakes violently—and 'earth' represents those aspects of the world which have physically reached their final expression after which they must be broken up, and mentally reached that state of fixation after which beliefs and dogmas, ideas and ideals must all be swept away by the invisible tide of truth. Is it not like an 'earthquake' when you look into your own mind, break free from illusion, realize enlightenment, teach truth, cease to obstruct Nirvana? We must meditate, not speculate, in order to come upon truth.

You may feel that the above has an Upanishadic bias, and that it does not tally with the belief of many Buddhists that Gotama freed himself from all Brahmanical influence and teaching, even that he rejected it as incorrect, especially in connection with the *ātman*. Let us look into this with a quiet, open mind. In the *Kītāgiri* and the *Caṇki Suttas* (*M*.1.480 and 2.173), the Buddha says: 'One who has faith draws close . . . sits down near by . . . and lends ear.' But this was precisely the Upanishadic way! It is the very meaning of the word *upanishad*! And that is not all, for the Buddha goes on to say: 'Lending ear he hears *Dhamma* . . . bears it in mind . . . tests the meaning . . . makes the effort . . . strives . . . and realizes with his person the highest truth itself, and penetrating it by means of wisdom, he sees.' But this precisely is the *śravaṇa, manana* and *nididhyāsana* of the *Adhyātma, Paingala, Nāradaparivrājaka* and other Upanishads! It is also, in essence, the way as laid down in the pre-Buddhistic major Upanishads.

Let us investigate more deeply, and fearlessly. In that revealing autobiographical discourse, the *Ariyapariyesana Sutta*, the Buddha says (*M*.1.167): 'Seeking the Unborn, the uttermost security from the bonds—*Nibbāna*—I won the Unborn, the uttermost security from the bonds—*Nibbāna*.' He repeats this formula again and again, substituting for the 'Unborn' the terms 'Unageing', 'Undecaying', 'Undying', 'Sorrowless', 'Unstained'.

Now listen to the pre-Buddhistic Upanishads. Yā jñavalkya says to King Janaka (*Brihadāraṇyaka Up.*, 4.4.25): 'This great unborn *ātman*, undecaying, immortal, fearless, is Brahman.' And to Kahola Kauśitakeya (*Brh. Up.*, 3.5): 'The *ātman* is that which transcends hunger and thirst, sorrow and delusion, old age and death.' In the *Chāndogya Upanishad* (8.1.5): 'That is the *ātman* which is sinless, ageless, deathless, sorrowless, hungerless and thirstless.' And the teacher, Prajāpati, says to Indra and Virocana (8.7.1.): 'The *ātman* which is sinless, ageless, deathless, sorrowless, hungerless, thirstless—'tis that which should be sought out.'

What other than the *ātman* was it that Siddhattha Gotama sought when he sought the unborn, the unageing, the undecaying, the undying, the unsorrowing, the unstained, for are not these the very terms in which the *ātman* was presented long before he was born?

Consider again what Yājñavalkya says to Śākalya, to Maitreyī and to King Janaka on separate occasions: 'That *ātman* is not this, it is not that. It is unseizable for it is not seized. It is indestructible for it is not worn out. It is the Alone for it is not attached to any thing. It is unbound. It does not tremble. It is not injured.' (*Brh. Up.* 3.9.26; 4.2.4; 4.4.22; 4.5.15.)

The *ātman* is not this, not that—not a stone or a flower, not an ant or an elephant, not anything you can know with your mind; not your body or feelings or ideas or consciousness. Did not the Buddha confirm all this when he taught with endless patience that the body, the feelings and so on, are 'not mine; these am I not; these are not the *atta* of me'? And did not the Buddha also say (*Udāna*, 8.3): '*Bhikkhus*, there is the not-born, not-become, not-made, not-compounded. If that un-born, not-become, not-made, not-compounded were not, there would be apparent no escape from this here that is born, become, made, compounded.' Are not these words of the Buddha his unequivocal affirmation of the Absolute, even as the terms of presentation of the Upanishadic *ātman* were the affirmations of the Absolute by the enlightened, liberated ones of Brahmanical India?

How comes it, then, that whereas Brahmanical teachings blazon forth the *Ātman* Doctrine, *anattā* is central to the Buddhist? The Upanishadic teachers sought answers to certain questions: What is the origin of the world as experienced by us? What is its relationship to that origin? Who or what are we? And what is our relationship to the Supreme Reality, and our ultimate destiny? They answered that it is the *ātman* which becomes the whole world. They went further and said that not only does the *ātman*, the One Reality, become the multitudinous variety, but also that it *is* this very variety. But this immediately raises a logical problem for us which seems insoluble. We see that all this, the world, is mortal, is in bondage and pain, is measurable and conditioned. How, then, can the *ātman* be unitary, immortal, infinite, unconditioned, absolute, and also be its opposite, namely multitudinous, mortal, finite, conditioned, relative?

The answer is simple to state, though difficult to comprehend. The finite and infinite, the mortal and immortal, are a non-duality. They appear to us to be irreconcilable opposites because we, not being fully awakened, are not effortlessly aware that the Totality is one, whole Reality. Not clearly seeing all relationships, we are conscious in separative terms. We are almost exclusively *thing*-conscious and unawake in the mode of *no-thing* consciousness, that is, of an all-pervasive field consciousness. When thing-consciousness and no-thing consciousness are integrated, unified as a non-duality, then there is *whole consciousness*, in which, among other things, there is no division into what is commonly termed the conscious and the unconscious.

The Upanishadic teachers also had another term for ultimate reality, namely Brahman, an objective term, the philosophical Absolute. They experienced its reality by going beyond the uttermost deep of their own consciousness. If Brahman were to announce itself and say 'I', that 'I' is the meaning of the term *ātman*, a subjective term. It is this subjective flavour which is responsible for using the word 'Self' (with a capital S) as the equivalent of *ātman*, despite the fact that it is a misleading word. What I have called *whole consciousness* is the pure or absolute consciousness which is the meaning of *ātman*, as in the *Varāha Upanishad* (2.20, 21). I also regard *ātman* as the eater-up of the mind. Now, when *no-thing consciousness* functions as freely as *thing-consciousness*, we are effortlessly awake to the complete relationships between all apparently separate entities and states of mind. Thereupon the mortal and the immortal, the finite and the infinite, are, for us, a non-duality, quite simply and factually, and love, the unifier and healer, is in full flower.

We must note carefully that the *ātman is*, but that the world *exists* dependently upon *ātman*. To exist (Latin, *ex-sistere*) means 'to come forth', 'to emerge', 'to appear out of'. The world appears out of, or is an appearance of, *ātman*. The unborn, undying *ātman* is the timeless, the immeasurable. The world is the born and the dying, the measurable, the incessantly changing. Whilst on the one hand the Upanishadic teachers declared that the *ātman* becomes, and is, all-this, on the other hand they designated all-this as not-*ātman*. They bridged the contradiction by presenting *ātman* as immanent in the form of things and also as transcendent in the formless no-thing. Yājñavalkya says to Uddālaka Āruni (*Brh. Up.* 3.7.3–23): 'He who, dwelling in the earth yet is other than the earth, whom the earth does not know, whose body the earth is, who controls the earth from within, He is your *ātman*, the Inner Controller, the Immortal.' This statement is repeated over and over again, substituting for the word 'earth', the words 'fire', 'sky', 'atmosphere', etc., in relation to the world, and the words 'life', 'speech', 'eye', 'ear', 'mind', etc., in relation to each person. Yājñavalkya ends his exposition thus: 'He the Seer is unseen, He the Hearer is unheard, He the Thinker cannot be conceived of, He the all-knower cannot be comprehended. There is no Seer, Hearer, Thinker or Knower but He. He is your Ātman, the Inner Controller, the Immortal. Everything else is of evil' (*ato'nyad ārtam*, which also means 'leading to misery, destruction, death').

Note the personalistic element in the presentation of the immanent *ātman*. Here is the stumbling block to understanding because of the tendency to picture it as an immortal entity, and in fact the Upanishads did talk of it as being 'of the size of a thumb . . . smaller than a grain of rice . . . greater than the earth', and as being 'seated in the heart'. The term 'immortal entity' is self-contradictory, for any entity is finite and, as such, it must of necessity come into being and cease to be. Those who, unlike Yājñavalkya, were still not fully enlightened, tended to identify this immanent *ātman*, pictured as a manikin soul, with the body, or with different states of consciousness, such as the dream state, the deep slumber state, etc. Their awareness was still largely confined to thing-consciousness. Hence the confusion, and the inability to realize the mortal and the immortal, the absolute and the relative as a non-duality.

This non-duality of the absolute and the relative is expressed in the *Prajñāpāramitā* literature and the Mādhyamika philosophy of Nāgārjuna as *śūnyatā*, emptiness. The germ of this lies in the Buddha's words to Kaccāyana (*Saṃyutta*, 2.15 and 3.135), where he points out that the world usually bases its views on two things, existence and non-existence. 'It is' and 'it is not' are the two extremes between which the world is imprisoned. But the Tathāgata teaches a *Dharma* that takes a middle way between them. This Dharma is presented in the Theravāda as the *paṭicca-samuppāda*, in the Mahāyāna as *śūnyatā*. The absolute is emptiness; all things are also empty. In their emptiness, Nirvana and this world coincide; Nirvana is not-different from birth-death, that is, from *saṃsāra*.

Śūnya is not a mere nothingness—bear this in mind, also, in relation to the Upanishadic *ātman*. *Śūnya* literally means 'relating to the swollen'. The root of *śūnya* is *śvi*, which seems to have expressed the idea that something which looks swollen from outside is hollow inside. If I may use an unusual expression, this inside hollowness of an outside swelling—and here you will get a feel of the meaning of *ākāśa*—is the emptiness. Not a mere nothing, not a blank, it is a term for the *absence of self*, for not-*ātman* or *anattā*. Both Nirvana and all things are *śūnya*, *anattā* as the texts put it.

Now consider very intently. Are they void of self, or, if I may so suggest, are they void of *self-ness*—of the conceptual self, which is self as we ordinarily imagine it? Is *anattā* absolutely no-*ātman*, or does it mean no *separate ātman*, no *my ātman* or *your ātman*, which would precipitate us into the obvious mistake of the manikin soul as an immortal entity, a self-contradictory term? Contemplate this—but contemplate it in the state of utter silence. Listen again with an open mind. The *ātman*—or the Buddha's unborn, undying, unbecome—transcends any changeless being or any ephemeral becoming. To transcend means to be wholly other than and yet not separate from. If you can see this, in you will arise the peaceful understanding that *ātman, śūnyatā*, deathlessness or Nirvana, all defeat the mind which is active in its stained condition. But when the mind is in equilibrium in its pure condition, it is in the state of Enlightenment with the unknowing knowing. Then there is Nirvana; but you the outside swelling with the hollow inside do not know it during the actual experiencing. It knows itself non-mentally. As I have said on other occasions, awareness and being are identical in transcendence.

His Holiness the XIVth Dalai Lama of Tibet says in his book, *The Opening of the Wisdom-Eye** (p. 70), that the teaching of *nairātmya, anattā*, is upheld by all schools of Buddhist thought, that the *ātman*-view, namely the belief in some permanent soul-entity, is the root of all trouble, and that it is because of the *ātman*-view that all beings are wandering on in the realm of *saṃsāra*. Please note very carefully the exact words: the *ātman*-view, according to Buddhist definition, is the belief in a permanent soul-entity. But this manikin soul, and all that is associated with it, the *skandhas* and *dharmas*, is precisely what the Upanishads called not-*ātman, anattā*. There is, in truth, no real dis-harmony between the Upanishads and the *Buddha-dharma*. The trouble arises only out of our own confusions and lack of clear insight, our own bias and prejudice and incomplete investigation.

Enough has been said to indicate that the misconception of *ātman* as a privately possessed immortal entity, a manikin soul, had spread in *brāhman* circles. When Siddhattha Gotama realized Enlightenment, he saw the situation clearly. The Transcendent Unborn, Unbecome, was that which was *ungraspable* and *inconceivable*, and

*Bangkok: Social Sciences Association of Thailand, 1968.

with which, in the words of the *Māṇḍukya Upanishad*, 'there could be no dealing'. There could only be silence in connection with it. But this, the faring—on through *saṃsāra*, was what we could deal with. So he taught the *Dharma* which he characterized as deep, difficult to see, tranquil, excellent, not to be understood by mere logic, subtle, but intelligible to the wise (*M*.1.167).

This *Dharma* is the *paṭicca-samuppāda*, causal uprising by way of conditions, or dependent origination. It presents the rationale of *dukkha*; it exposes the mechanism of *saṃsāra*; it shows the uprising and extinguishing of the whole mass of *dukkha*. Where the diagnosis is right, the cure is at hand. What the Buddha called *dukkha*, the Upanishads called *bandha*, 'bondage'. The *Sarvasāra Upanishad* says: 'The *ātman* (the unborn, undying, unstained), identified with the body personally, or with any manifestation universally, is bondage. Freedom from such identification is liberation. That which causes this identification is ignorance (the unawakened state); that which removes this identification is wisdom (the awakened state).' Indeed, then, the Buddha taught the way to liberation when he taught *anattā*.

Now Sāriputta lays down (*M*.1.54) that ignorance, the first and basic factor of the *paṭicca-samuppāda*, is the not-knowing of the Four Noble Truths. Since ignorance is the main root of suffering or of bondage, and since wisdom, the awakened state, is the foundation of Nirvana or Liberation, the whole of *dukkha* or of *bandha* is most intimately concerned with the mind. The texts clearly show (e.g. *M.A.* 1.223 f.) that *saṃsāra* as the universal becoming-process has no beginning or ending. Yet the *dukkha* afflicting our minds individually can be extinguished, whereupon our *saṃsāra*, purified of all stains, is suffused with Nirvana. *Dukkha* and its cause, craving, announced in the first two Noble Truths, lie in the worldly context of mortality. The third and fourth Noble Truths, the extinction of *dukkha* which spells Nirvana and the Eightfold Path, belong to the transcendent context. The Eightfold Path is the perfect way—and perfection is transcendent. The Mahāyāna presentation of the path points to this rather more than the Theravāda does. The Eightfold Path is the complement in the transcendent context of the *paṭicca-samuppāda* in the worldly context. The Buddha, like all other great teachers, gave the transcendent answer to all worldly problems.

Much lies hidden in the open words of the teachings. Let us consider the fourth factor in the *paṭicca-samuppāda*, viz. *nāma-rūpa*, usually translated as 'name-shape', as 'mind-body' and as 'materiality-mentality'. *Nāma*, mind, is explained (e.g. in the *Visuddhimagga*, 17.187, and in the *Abhidhamma*) as the three *khandhas* or aggregates of feelings, perceptions and mental formations or states.

How does the Vedānta present *nāma-rūpa*? Brahman, the Absolute, through *māyā*, the illusion-making power, gives rise to Brahmā, the creator. Both the creator and his creation are the product of *avidyā*, ignorance, for all creation is but the ephemeral thought or dream of the creator. As such, it constitutes the whole realm of *dukkha*. And yet at the same time, with that charming illogicality which has its own say in creation myths, knowledge is the only predicate which all religions ascribe to the creator. If one asks what are the objects of knowledge, or the thoughts of Brahmā, the answer is 'names and forms', the *nāma-rūpe*. Up to a point these are similar to the Ideas of Plato, the *species* of the later Stoics, the *samjñā dharmas* of the Buddhists (*Sacred Books of the East*, Vol. 49, p. 117), the *Logos* that was called by Philo, long before St John, the *Alone-Begotten*. The *nāma-rūpe* were the creative *logoi*; the gods such as Agni, ruler of earth, Vāyu of air, Sūrya of sky; the archetypes. Brahman the Absolute communicates by means of names and forms with this universe which extends as far as name and form extend. The Buddha refers to these Vedic gods, Sakka (Indra), Prajāpati, Brahmā Sahampati and the whole host of them who are but ephemeral *nāma-rūpe*, for they are born and they cease to be.

In the Upanishads, Ārtabhaga asks (*Brh. Up.*, 3.2.12): 'When a man dies, what does not leave him?' And Yājñavalkya answers: 'The name. Endless, verily is the name, and endless are the All-gods.' What does 'name' mean in this context? Might it be an informing principle, an archetype? The Sufi poet Rūmī says (*Shams-i-Tabriz*, XII): 'Every shape you see has its archetype.' The mediaeval European *forma* corresponds closely to the Indian notion of *nāma*, which is the noumenal, intelligible cause of the integration constituting each individual in its finite limitations.

Now the whole process of liberation entails the complete negation of this world, the complete reversal of the ordinary human condition (viz. *dukkha* and the darkness of ignorance, the unawakened state). But you cannot negate the world as a physical fact. The enlightened and the ignorant alike do live, and have to live, *in* the world. The negation is the negation of the world as conceived by the unenlightened mind, and it takes place in the mind as one enters deeper and deeper into the *jhānas*, the profounder states of consciousness, steadily disentangling oneself from all forms. *Rūpa* is *ākāśa* constrained into illusory forms, and *nāma* is mind inclining to *rūpa*; and the interlocking of these two with *viññāṇa* is the existential being, you or I, he or she. In the deep *samāpattis*, the constrained *ākāśa* and *viññāṇa* are freed into their natural state of infinity, and *nāma* and *rūpa* vanish as obstructors to wisdom. As one goes deeper into No-thing, all the archetypes and all the gods dissolve. They exist only as long as the beliefs and memories and devotions of men in the unenlightened state give them continuity in the mind. As the Tibetans say: Gods, demons, the whole universe, are but a mirage which exists in the mind, springs from it and sinks into it. And in that delightful discourse entitled 'A Challenge to a Brahmā' (*Brahmānimantanika Sutta*, M.1.326–331), the Buddha reveals this same truth to him who has eyes to see. It is the conceptualizing mind which paints the picture of spiritual beings and forces, and all the furniture of heaven and hell. The concept *tree* is not the actual tree perceived in the immediate, living *here-now*. The movement through the *jhānas* sweeps the mind clean of the mountainous heap of concepts, of vain beliefs and fixed ideas, of age-old powerful archetypal images, and of any and every idol of divinity however exalted in our fond fantasy. But this can happen truly and without self-deception, and happen safely, only if there is the firm basis of pure morality.

And then you will know death—not death the deliverer of the wages of sin, but death the perfector and consummator. You will know it peacefully and fearlessly, and for the first time in your life you will be filled with the wonder of creative renewal. For when the mind is pure, empty, transparent, luminous, then egoistic self-consciousness is no more. Instead, there is what the Buddha called *viññāṇaṃ anidassanaṃ anantaṃ sabbato pabham*: 'the awareness which is attributeless, unending, shining everywhere'. Such a mind is perfectly clear-seeing, for it offers no obstruction to the free functioning of the liberated intelligence. Free of all stains, wholly attentive without any grasping to the flow of life *here-now*, you are free of psychological time and all the sorrow it holds. The timeless eternal, because of your fully-awakened state, is embodied in every moving flicker of time. Therefore every instantaneous birth, that is, every uprisen state of mind—is completely worked out, leaving no residue whatsoever. This means that you die wholly to every fleeting moment whilst alive in the body.

Where there is the perfect rhythm of birth and death, you see the dance of life. You experience the deathless state, the Nirvana that is never born, nor ages, nor dies. You enjoy the rose of your salvation under the light of heaven.

Götterdämmerung

(1970)

LET US concern ourselves with the twilight of the gods. Born in the dawn of psychological time, they rule the bond slaves of ignorance and craving till the long night of the cosmos lays them to rest in the oblivion of sleep. We cannot ignore them or dismiss them out of vain conceit or pride. But whoever is enlightened can go beyond them all.

The gods are many. There are the evil gods: Māra the deceiver and death dealer, and his hosts; craving, discontent and passion; ambition and envy; fear and hate; and power-lust that spells wars and cruel oppression. Send them to their doom, and the forces of evil are impotent against you. There are the mischievous gods of the everyday world: success and security; money and pleasure; worldly culture and self-aggrandisement. Put them aside, and you walk out of the prison of self-orientation and separateness.

There are the celestials: the Brahmās, the Four Great Kings, the Thirty-three *Devas*, the Yāma *Devas* and many others, including the *devas* of the planes of form and formlessness that are associated with the *jhānas* and the *samāpattis*. The Buddha tells the *brāhman* youth Saṅgārava of the Bhāradvāja clan (*M*.ii.212): 'Certainly, it is known to me that there are *devas*. There are also other gods, harsh jailers exercising oppressive sway over us: doctrine, dogma, belief, conviction; prejudice, bias, preconception, assumption; idea, ideal; knowledge, philosophy; thought, experience, memory and others of all that brood. The "I-am" conceit is their father; unenlightenment their mother.

Light up the darkness, slough away the conceit, and unshakable freedom of mind is yours.'

Purely for convenience let us use this word 'gods', in a very loose sense, to include strictly-defined terms such as *issara,* a creator deity; *devas,* a term applied to certain human and non-human beings and, according to Buddhist teachings, mortal and subject to *kamma;* to include sorrow-begetting gods, such as golden calves and self-indulgence; to include the high gods of several pantheons, the deities and angelic hierarchies of various religions; and also to include the archetypal forms and forces in various teachings. Judaism, Christianity and Islam state that the archangelic and angelic orders were created by God. In Zarathushtrianism, the Ameshāṣpands are the creation of Ahurā-Mazdā. The *Rig Veda* calls the high gods the children of Aditi, the Unbound or Infinite. The *Śatapatha Brahmaṇa* states that Brahman creates Agni, Vāyu and Sūrya, and makes them lords of earth, air and sky, and itself goes beyond. Then Brahman returns again by means of name and form; and as far as name and form extend, so far does the universe extend. The Hindus have hosts of *devas,* celestial as well as demonic; the Buddha takes them as a matter of course. Even as Hinduism presents the gods with their consorts, Buddhism presents Dhyāni Buddhas with their consorts.

You, the human being, are the progenitor of the gods, be they high gods, celestials, mischievous gods or demons. When you yourself, in deep meditation, are beyond duality, in that unified state where there is no obtrusive 'I-am' conceit, there is only transcendent awareness. When all evil-mindedness has been burnt out, you are the holy one. When you are in that silent communion where there is the cessation of perception and feeling, the One Total Reality is manifest as realized Transcendence through you. This is the state of the one-only, not-born, not-becoming, not-dying. Free of any separate self-consciousness, you are awake to the fact that Transcendence, pure mind and the natural world are in timeless conjugation. In course of time, there is the return journey to ordinary, discriminative consciousness, and once again you are in the realm of the many.

It is during this return journey that the creation by you of your psycho-spiritual cosmos takes place, and the One proliferates and becomes the many, taking the shapes made by the interpretive activity of your discriminative consciousness, in accordance with its conditioning by your cultural heritage.

Thereafter, you the holy one may try to communicate the experiencing of Transcendence to earnest learners in terms of God, and/or the high gods. This communication, which purports to be the knowledge of the nature and functioning of the transcendent cosmic energy which is presented as God or as the high gods, is the meaning of the word 'Theosophy'. The strictest and finest Theosophy is the unwritten Revelation: the Qabalah, of which there are formal expressions such as the books of Moses, the writings of the Qabalists, the Zohar, etc.; the original Veda, of which the formal expressions are the written Vedas, the Upanishads, etc.; the primordial *Buddha-dharma,* which was re-lit in our world-age by the historical Buddha through his utterance of the *brahmavāda*. You the holy one may also try to convey Transcendence as Brahman-*ātman*; as the not-born, not-becoming, not-dying; as *śūnyatā*; as Nirvana; as Godhead; as the divine dark; as the Absolute.

Recall the statement made earlier: *Transcendence, pure mind and the natural order are in timeless conjugation*. They mutually fecundate each other. The impress of Transcendence upon pure mind is interpreted by the holy one as the archetypal forces. Plato, for example, presented them as the Ideas—Truth, Goodness, Beauty; others have presented them as the laws governing the spiritual life; others, as spiritual hierarchies in charge of cosmic and human evolution. Although pure mind is formless, the psyche, conditioned by one's particular cultural heritage and environment imaginatively clothes the impress of Transcendence upon pure mind in various forms—a wonderful psychological key for understanding oneself and one's race.

We must now consider a crucial point. Transcendence is *nitya,* that is, it is absolute, immeasurable, indestructible, unconditioned. Neither space nor time nor causality nor process apply to it. The only words we can use in connection with it are those which deny or negate our whole system of knowledge, which is dependent upon the workings of our senses and discriminative consciousness, *viññāṇa*. Transcendence is the unknown and unknowable. *I* cannot touch or know or experience Transcendence. But if I empty myself, if there is no self-ness, then this very self is wholly transparent to the light of Transcendence.

Pure mind, also, is immeasurable. *Ākāśa* is mind-space, space devoid of separation and distances, devoid of time and of the usual dimensions of physical space of which we are conscious through our *viññāṇa*. It is self-shining—its shining is the 'light' of Transcendence. Pure mind and Transcendence are formless. On rare occasions, the activity of our *viññāṇa* seems to reach out into the formless and immeasurable, and then it inevitably interprets Transcendence and pure mind in the terms of its known limitations and categories, such as space, time, finite particulars and so on; in other words, in terms of form and the movement of successive events; i.e., in terms of birth and death, of the relative, *anicca*. This is our crucial point; this is where our difficulty lies. We are driven to represent the infinite in the figure of the finite. Furthermore, being in the state of ignorance (*avidyā*), we tend to believe, and to act on the belief, that our formal representations are the truth, the reality; and we fail to be awake to the fact that they are all illusory where Transcendence and pure mind are concerned.

The religious life is concerned with the realization of Transcendence. This necessitates a basis of pure conduct of body, speech and thought in daily life. It involves the purification and emptying of the mind and a complete transformation of the mode of awareness of that which is, *here-now*. This means a total release from the *saṃsāric* mode into the Nirvanic. To this end, we have to see and to live by the fact that our existential self or being, the *nāma-rūpa*, is relative (*anicca*), not transcendent (*anattā*), far from the infinite (*dukkha*). If this is done, it means that we are unselfed, or, that we are ego-less beings. Then indeed we are true humans.

Let us now consider some difficulties. We believe that we can look objectively or dispassionately at a person or thing. In actual fact our looking is tainted with greed, hatred and delusion. So too is our hearing, touching, etc.; so too our planning, investigating, feeling, aspiring, worshipping and striving. We believe we can distinguish what is good and true. But if we are really mindful we continuously discover that our capacity for distinguishing correctly is woefully short. What we actually do is grasp at an idea, a feeling, a pattern of thought. In short, the entire functioning of our *viññāṇa*, our discriminative consciousness, is tainted throughout with greed, hatred and delusion.

Thus, even when we try to tread the path, or imagine we are doing so, we are still in miserable servitude to the gods. If we are mindful, we will see that we are still self-orientated, still pleasure-bent, still grasping at Nirvana or Buddhahood and deluded as to the significance and meaning of those words. We give them meanings and form conceptions about them out of our dead past. So strong is the drive of craving that we struggle with might and main to win by force our pictured Transcendence, a mere *saṇkhāra*. And we continue in this state of conflict and woe, blind to the fact that we are caught in the web of words, a web of our own making.

The release from the trap of words and servitude to the gods is effected in the *jhānas* and *samāpattis*, in which a progressive dissolution of all thought patterns and verbal structures, such as beliefs, assumptions, doctrines, laws and so on, takes place. A *jhāna* (Skt. *dhyāna*) is a state of attentiveness. Ordinarily, we are in a state of confusion; our attention is like a straw in the wind. In the first *jhāna* there is an orderly movement of discursive thought. Dhammadinna, the nun, tells Visākha (*M*.1.301), 'Discursive thought is activity of speech.' This speech is a flow of the known or the past, a flow of thought-forms shaped and structured by the tainted *viññāṇa*. Among these thought-forms or verbal structures are the usual set topics for meditation, and the process of the meditation is a modified continuity of what is already known. Very rarely is the really new present—your flash of inspiration, the forward step. The thought-forms are fixations. We hold on to them and they become hindrances.

In the second *jhāna*, the flow of discursive thought (which is speech) becomes quiescent. So also does the flow of internal sense impressions—visual, auditory, tactile etc.—all of which, at root, are associated with words. And thus you experience the first death. It is essential to understand this.

Consider carefully the significance of the word. With very rare exceptions, all words represent a thing or action or quality, etc., each of which is limited, finite and particular: it comes into being, changes and perishes: it is cognized through the medium of our senses and brain by the tainted and unenlightened *viññāṇa*, discriminative consciousness, which by the very fact of discrimination takes sides, perpetuates conflict and is always fragmentary—therefore you are never wholly one with truth, with the One Total Reality. Thus words represent the realm of duality and mortality. Therefore, when the flow of speech and sense impressions is quiescent whilst you are awake and fully attentive, not asleep or dead, a new dimension of being and consciousness stirs out of the depths of the mind and you are aware of a far profounder life, which is speechless. This is the first and in some respects the most important transformation of the mode of awareness. Hitherto you were fragmentarily aware in the mode of mortality. Now you are beginning to realize the unified mind, so that the *viññāṇa*, becoming more free of its defilements, begins to apprehend things and persons and situations in their wholeness.

Now Buddhist cosmology is of the mind-world, not of the physical world like our modern scientific cosmologies. It is a psycho-cosmic system. The Buddhist universe of mind deals with fact, the reality of which depends on its *psychological* truth and the possibility of its experience in one or other state of consciousness. This may or may not include materiality in association with mentality. We must be prepared then, conditioned as we are by our modern education, to meet with a strangeness in the verbal formulation of this psycho-cosmic system. We must bear in mind that all the heavens and hells, together with their denizens, are within our minds as possibilities of consciousness. We classify and name these immaterial beings in accordance with our socio-cultural heritage. In India we call them *devas*. In the Judaeo-Christian and Islamic traditions they are called archangels and angels, but with this difference, that, in contrast to the Indian view, they are regarded as created by God and as immortal, and not as beings who are subject to death, or who are creations of our own minds.

The psycho-cosmic system of Buddhism presents three realms: that of sensuous desire (*kāmaloka*), of pure form (*rūpaloka*), and of the formless (*arūpaloka*). In the *jhānas*, attention is centred in the realm of pure form. Although the *jhānas* are designated as first, second, third and fourth, do not regard them as if they were rungs on a ladder. It is more as if you were in an envelope of water, or of air: the more profound the *jhāna*, the less the fluctuation of the mind in this realm of pure form, a realm of mind-forms, and the envelope of water or air is less disturbed by currents. The number attached to any *jhāna* indicates its intensity and nature.

Five important factors characterize the first *jhāna* state: 1. specifically directed attention to the subject in hand, brought back again and again if the mind wanders (*vitakka*)—this removes sloth and torpor (*thīna-middha*); 2. sustained attention (*vicāra*); which removes doubt (*vicikicchā*)—distinguish this doubt, mere cavilling or cantankerous opposition out of folly or vanity, from that healthy doubt which impels us to serious investigation; 3. rapture (*pīti*) which removes hate (*dosa* or *byāpāda*); 4. happiness (*sukha*) which removes restlessness and mental worry (*uddhacca-kukkucca*); 5. and single-mindedness, usually called one-pointedness (*ekaggatā*), which removes greed (*lobha*).

As you move closer to the single-minded state, each of the first four factors fades away, and the demon associated with each—sloth, doubt etc.—is consigned to limbo. By the going down of former pleasure and sorrow, you enter upon and abide in the fourth *jhāna*, which is entirely purified by mindfulness and equanimity. In this state there is freedom from separative self-consciousness. There is no I-association with any of the constituents of being, bodily or mental. Thus the true meaning of the word 'I', freed from 'I-am' conceit, is realized.

The Buddha constantly uses the word *ahaṃ*, I. We generally use it to signify something relative or ephemeral, as when we remark, 'I am hungry or tall or elated.' Here the fact is that there is hunger or tallness or elation apparent for the time being. According to the ancient wisdom, *ahaṃ* signifies that reality which cannot be denied after the sense of separate selfhood, of an I-entity, is dissolved. *Ahaṃ* is the unabandonable. If we see this, there is realization that the 'I' is in fact the One Total Reality manifesting itself as innumerable, finite, self-cognizing forms. Thus, when one who is well awake to this fact uses the word 'I', that I refers to the one and only universal I, of which the existential being or the *nāma-rūpa* known in the world by one's name is a focus of manifestation.

The attentiveness of the fourth *jhāna*, entirely purified by mindfulness and equanimity, is a state of silence, a silence which absorbs all sound without being perturbed. Its *upekkhā*, equanimity, is such that it is the culmination of love—that is, of *mettā, karuṇā* and *muditā*—and it is a peace which allows awareness to be whole, not merely analytical or separative. It is free of conflict, for it does not take sides or indulge in preferential choice. In the fourth *jhāna* you are in the unresisting state; the mind is pliable, clean and empty of all the thought-forms which are raised up by the activity of desire. In this state, craving cannot reach you, for with the quiescence of separate self-consciousness, self-centred desire cannot act. With craving gone, there cannot be an uprising, another *jāti* (a conditioned state). Being in the unconditioned state, being free of the flow of discursive speech and thought and sense images, unobstructed *prajñā*, that is, unerring insight, operates in your awareness. Thus with *prajñā* and *karuṇā* functioning freely through you in *upekkhā*, you realize another death—death the liberation out of the finitude of the five aggregates, out of the limitations of *viññāṇa*, into the infinitude of pure mind.

This is the entry into the *samāpattis*, or coalescences. The organism which is 'you', in silent stillness, is now in the mindless state. This means that what is commonly called 'my' mind or 'your' mind, which in fact is merely the ephemeral flow of mental patterns, having become empty, and because there is perfect ease and poise, is utterly transparent and shining—it is the All-mind, *ākāśa* the mind-space, shining with the light of transcendence. This mind-space has no dimensions geometrically: no length, no depth, no breadth; it is not measurable in terms of finitude. But it is immeasurably full in terms of archetypal forces, fecundated as it is by transcendence; and its dimensions are in terms of the fullness, that is, the intensity, of pure consciousness. The infinity of *ākāśa* necessarily implies the infinity of *viññāṇa*. When there is the seeing of the fullness of emptiness, only then is there the seeing of the emptiness; and pure consciousness is the fullness of the emptiness.

The movement out of the fourth *jhāna* and the entry and abiding in the infinity of *ākāśa* and *viññāṇa* takes place, as the Buddha teaches, 'by passing quite beyond perception of material shapes, by the going down of perception of sensory reactions, by not attending to perception of variety'. This statement is very important. For it means that in the sphere of infinity, all discriminative perception ceases. The requisite bases of *viññāṇa*—space, time, separation, measurability—have all disappeared. This unconditioned, uniformly calm realm, is the realm of primordial creative action by that aspect of cosmic energy which is called the Power of God the incomprehensible deity, of Brahman or *atman*, the Unknown Infinite, in the esoteric teachings of various religions. (In this connection, see the *Mahāvagga*, 1.6.37–41; and the *Saṃyutta Nikāya*, 3.67.) This unfolding of the unknown Transcendence in infinity, displaying the movement of divine power, is the essential subject-matter of Theosophy. But how shall *viññāṇa*, especially the tainted *viññāṇa* of mortals imprisoned in the circle of death (viz., the *paticca-samuppāda* from *avidyā* to *jarā-maraṇa*), ever talk about the ways of God or the workings of Transcendence, and try to fit them into the finite framework upreared by *viññāṇa*? Out of his great compassion, the Buddha taught us that investigation was one of the limbs of enlightenment; and he also taught the indispensability of the foundation of pure morality. Beware then of the lure of power-lust as a motive force impelling us to investigate. Leave alone all power. It is invariably and inevitably misused until every vestige of taint is out of your mind and heart, and the harmony of transcendent love and wisdom flows in a healing stream out of your unselfed being for the joy and the peace of all mankind. And in the infinity of *ākāśa* and *viññāṇa*, transcendent love and wisdom *will* flood your being and radiate into the world.

Before we proceed further, let us go back to the beginning and pick up another thread. As you outgrow the life of slavery to sense pleasure, you move out of *kāmaloka*, the state of confinement to sensuous living. In its higher reaches are included the *devas* collectively called the Four Great Kings, the Thirty-three Gods and so on. You go beyond them till in the first *jhāna* you come to the Great Brahmā (Mahā-Brahmā) and his ministers and retinues; in the second, to the *devas* of minor, infinite and radiant lustre (*parittābhā, appamāṇābhā, ābhassarā*); in the third, to the *devas* of minor, infinite and steady aura (*parittasubhā, appamāṇasubhā, subhakiṇṇa*); and in the fourth, to the *devas* of the realm of great reward (*vehapphalā*), of mindless being (*asaññasattā*) and of the pure abodes (*suddhāvāsā*). This last includes the durable, serene, beautiful, clear-sighted and the highest realms with their respective *devas* (*avihā, atappā, sudassī, sudassā* and *akaṇitthā*). You may wonder who or what *are* these *devas*, corporeal and non-corporeal. It may be helpful, in this connection, to study Discourses 1, 37, 49 and 50 in the *Majjhima Nikāya*. But the wise man will concern himself less with a verbal answer to the question and more with understanding the nature of curiosity. If you meet with *devas*, be grateful for any wisdom you may cull, but do not grasp at anything. Remain circumspect.

As you move through the *jhānas* to your in-gathering into reality, you will become free of bondage to the gods. The process culminates in the third *samāpatti*, the plane of no-thing. Note that all this is not just another mode of ordinary thinking; not mere words. It is a transformation of awareness, the awareness which implies *being that which you are aware of*. In other words, the separation between seeing subject and object is vanishing and there is a coalescence of the two. Verbal statements become increasingly inept as you go on; they are made only because we are trying to communicate with each other. In no-thing awareness, the deeply hidden mental impressions, the inherited archetypal images and the ingrained natural urges derived from the animal origin of the body and of that part of the psyche associated with it, all dissolve away. For here the culmination of mindfulness, *satipaṭṭhāna*, takes place. In daily practice, all the components of the existential being were seen with right wisdom to be relative, not transcendent, sorrowful, and you said of each of them, 'this is not mine, this am I not, this is not the *attā* of me'. So you did not grasp at them. In no-thing, there is no intrusion upon awareness by any of these.

Now, there is the dissolution of all your ideals, of all your rigid, misleading thought-forms in which *viññāṇa* structured ungraspable, formless truth, of your paths to Enlightenment and your pictured Enlightenment itself; of your high gods, who represented all that mortals call best and perfect; of your firmest convictions that the true and good and beautiful are eternal and indestructible—all of it will vanish in that no-thing which is the very 'substance' of the infinite. The Buddha said to Sāriputta: '"Bodhisattva", "perfect wisdom", "form" etc., are mere words . . . magical illusions. They are not, do not arise, are false to behold' (Conze: *Selected Sayings from the Perfection of Wisdom*, p. 97). And to Subhuti: 'Enlightenment is attained neither through a path nor through a no-path. Just the path is enlightenment, just enlightenment is the path' (*ibid.*, p. 115).

Most awesome of all is the realization that the power of Transcendence acts as a rhythmic pulse of destruction-regeneration. It shatters whatsoever is formed and established and reduces it to its primordial nothingness; and it fecundates this thing-less mind-space with life-energy from which springs forth the new cosmos; so the night of dissolution is followed by the dawn of new creation. Neither fear the night nor cling to the day. Nor hold your head high in pride before the Transcendent Power, but let your whole being burn with outstreaming love and wisdom in selfless living.

Stay still now, for there is yet a slight oscillation, an inclining towards an unperceivable *that* and a withdrawing into a perceiving self. It is a faint tremble of fear. Give way to it and you will be flung back into limited self-consciousness by a dark, tumultuous confusion. Stay still, for beyond the topmost summit of becoming is the cessation (*nirodha*), the cessation of the relative, the state of bondage. Then, there is only the light of Transcendence. Liberated from the grasp of flesh, Psyche is now one with Eros, the Eros which is Transcendence creating, in timeless conjugation with pure mind and nature; not that Eros which confused, impure mortals know.

And with the twilight of the gods, the world is redeemed by love and liberated by wisdom; and heaven's benediction restores to earth its pristine fragrance.

The Star and the Bubble

(1972)

SUVIKRANTAVIKRAMIN said: 'All beings are desirous of happiness, but outside wisdom we do not see, O Lord, any happiness for any being. Apart from the mode of life of the Bodhisattvas, there is nowhere any happiness for any being.'

The Buddha declared: 'In agreement with reality is this enlightenment of a Buddha. The thought of beings of inferior resolve does not stride in sublime *dharmas*, in *Buddhadharmas*. Those who are of inferior resolve, and conceited, abide in a condition which is contrary to the Enlightenment of a Buddha. They cannot understand the deep Dharma. What could "Beggarly beings" do with the precious Dharma, beings destitute of learning, or confused by their learning, beings who are but blind fools? The heretics of other sects . . . and all the foolish common people are "beggarly beings", all those who have sunk into the mud of false views . . . who treat the data of experience as signs of realities, who have strayed on to a wrong path . . . It is not possible, O Subhuti, that this discourse of Dharma could be learned by beings of inferior resolve, or by . . . beings who have not taken the pledge of Bodhisattvas.'

Only those who have taken the Bodhisattva Vow can learn the Dharma! When the Buddha asked Sariputra if it occurred to the *srāvakas* and *pratyekabuddhas* to think that, after they had known full enlightenment they should lead all beings into the realm of Nirvana which leaves nothing behind, *Parinirvāna*, Sariputra answered, 'No indeed, O

Lord'. 'But such indeed', said the Buddha, 'are the intentions of the *Bodhisattva*.' And he went on to add that the light of the glow-worm, like that of the *srāvakas* and *pratyekabuddhas*, cannot illumine a great continent, whereas the light of the risen sun, like that of the *Bodhisattvas*, can do so. A stark comparison!

It would not profit us to speculate whether the comparison is justifiable or not, or whether it was even made by the Buddha himself. For us, it is pertinent and urgent to ask ourselves seriously why we turn to religion, and to find out if we have any understanding of the implications of living the religious life.

Why do we turn to religion? Is it because we are hurt? Sorrowful? Frustrated? Frightened? Battered and defeated? Or is it because we are conceited—crazy enough to be militant evangelists, for this is the only field in which we can dominate others and inflate our own ego? Is it because we are confused and ignorant, see no meaning or purpose in life and would like an answer? Or is it a self-indulgence in emotional and intellectual pleasure—something to flaunt in our social circle? A status symbol, perhaps? We must ask ourselves all these questions and find out the answers from within ourselves. Let there be no illusions about our motives. Each and every self-orientated approach to religion is false and self-defeating. It makes us agents of greater ill.

What are the implications of living the religious life? In a sentence, the complete reversal of all worldliness; we have to grow out of our sub-human condition into the truly human state. In practice this means the Middle Way, which is perfect asceticism—that is, putting away whatever obstructs the realization of the Unconditioned. It means freedom from all self-indulgence, violence, ambition and ill-will; from fear, restlessness and stupidity. It means constant mindfulness and clear perception of the fact as it actually is. It means one must never attempt to grasp or to fixate the becoming-process but allow it to flow past—and this, too, is the meaning of asceticism. It means the life of meditation, which includes all right action. It means abiding in friendliness and compassion. It means perfect communion. Is it surprising, then, that Sakra said:

'This Dharma is wonderful, O Lord, it is astonishing, O Well-gone! As contrary to the whole world is this Dharma demonstrated. It has been preached so that *dharmas* should not be taken up. Yet the world is determined to take up *dharmas.*'

If the questions we have asked ourselves regarding our motives are satisfactorily answered and the implications of the religious life are lived in daily practice, we will see that the context of religion is transcendence, the Unconditioned, and that the spiritual life is rooted in and begins with saintliness. He who has dispelled sense-illusions and seen through the elemental compositeness of all conditioned things and states, realizes the Unconditioned, Nirvana. He is like a star, for he is a self-shining light.

If we are close enough to a star, that star shines for us like the sun: a source of light and life and love. If we are not close enough, we see a point of light amongst a host of twinkles, an uplifting and inspiring wonder and delight. But the host of twinkles cannot support our life as our sun does.

A buddha is like a star. What is the measure, if measure there be, of our closeness to him? Our purity, our whole purity. Then there is no dust in our space—the Void is transparent: our eyes are not on fire—vision is true: and we see the light itself—a miracle!—and not only the objective being reflecting the light.

Like a star is the Tathāgata, the Arahant, the Holy One, the Bodhisattva! Like a star is the *Prajñāpāramitā*! The oldest text of the *Prajñāpāramitā,* usually translated as 'Perfect Wisdom', is the version in 8,000 lines, the *Aṣṭasāhasrikā,* which probably dates back to 100 BC. Here it is written that the Lord said: 'Perfect Wisdom is the mother and begetter of the Tathāgatas; she showed them all-knowledge; she instructed them in the ways of the world. From her have the Tathāgatas come forth. For she has begotten and shown the cognition of the all-knowing (*Sarvajñatā*), she has shown the world for what it really is. The all-knowledge of the Tathāgatas has come forth from her. All the Tathāgatas, past, future and present, win full enlightenment thanks to this perfection of wisdom. And it is in this sense that the perfection of wisdom generates the Tathāgatas, and instructs them in the world.'

Furthermore, the Buddha said: 'Thanks to this lore, all Buddhas know full Enlightenment. Thanks to this lore, all the wholesome ways of action, the *jhānas* and *samāpattis* upheld by the limbs of enlightenment, the superknowledges associated with the limbs of enlightenment, in short all the articles of Dharma, the cognition of the Buddha, of the Self-Existent, the inconceivable cognition, all these become manifest in the world . . . It is perfect wisdom which appeases all evil and does not increase it, beginning with ordinary greed up to the attempt to seize on Nirvana as one's own personal property.'

The *Prajña-pāramitā Sutra* is thought of as a treatise on the wisdom that transcends, or the wisdom that is gone beyond. In this connection, Harold Talbott has written: 'The *Prajñāpāramitā Sutra* is the key document of the Mahāyāna, treating of Emptiness and the Wisdom Which Has Gone Beyond. It has denied the validity of all statements in the Buddhist scriptures, has insisted that the Buddha deliberately spoke about what he knew to be transcendent, not only to speech but to thought itself. Anyone who aspires to Buddhahood sees that all the doctrine and practice of Buddhism is an error, a charade, and a distraction from awareness of the truth . . . What does the *Prajñāpāramitā* suggest in place of the tenets which have been criticized out of existence? The answer is, of course, nothing, for, say the Mādhyamika philosophers (the *Śūnyavādins*), we will point out the emptiness of your religious or philosophical replacements. Is emptiness, then, to replace the criticized totality of religion and philosophy? Certainly not. Here is what the Mādhyamikas say about the notion of Emptiness:

> Form is empty in respect to emptiness;
> Emptiness is empty in respect to form;
> Emptiness is empty in respect to the distinction between form and emptiness, and
> Emptiness is empty in respect to emptiness.

Well then, what about replacing religion and philosophy with the *Wisdom Gone Beyond*, the *Prajñāpāramitā* itself?

'Here the Tibetans have made a wonderful contribution . . . The *Prajñnapāramitā*, say the Tibetan Masters, is not to be thought of as Wisdom Which Has Gone Beyond, not as the wisdom that transcends: it is referred to as that which transcends wisdom. That is Vajrayāna and Sahajayāna: naturally and fearlessly dwelling, free of attachment to thoughts, in the *Mañdala* of spontaneously arising and dissolving forms. Don't get *stuck* in "transcendence", in other words—otherwise it won't be transcendence.'

The *Prajñāpāramitā*, not dependent upon anything, is a self-shining light, a star. So, too, the Tathāgata is a star. For the Tathāgata is 'incapable of deliberately taking life; of taking, with the intention of stealing, what is not given: of indulging in carnal intercourse; of intentionally telling a lie; of enjoying pleasures from savings, as when he was a householder. With the destruction of the cankers, he is incapable of going the way of desire, hate, delusion and fear.' The Tathāgata is termed 'recluse, *brāhman*, discoverer, healer, stainless, pure, knower, freed, wholly awakened'.

The Buddha said: 'The Tathāgata speaks in accordance with reality, speaks the truth, speaks thus and not otherwise. The Tathāgata does not speak falsely.' The Tathāgata's speech is gentle, appealing and beneficial, mild, knowledgeable and mind-delighting. The Buddha is free of the fear of robbers or animals, whether in city or forest. He never forgets what has to be done by him. His mind is always well-established in voidness, never separated from penetration into the nature of reality. The rain of his friendliness and compassion falls steadily and continuously upon suffering beings. He has attained the freedom in which there is the cessation of all obstructions and he can never fall from this state of freedom.

The Buddha knows directly, not by way of reflection or speculation, all that constitutes our sense-mind functioning. This is his all-knowing knowledge (*sarvajñā-jñāna*), for which he is called the All-knower. He dwells continually in friendliness and compassion. He is embodied *mahā-prajñā* and *mahā-karuñā*.

What exactly is the Tathāgata? A being—or not a being? As to this, the Lord said:

Those who by my form did see me,
And those who followed me by my voice.
Wrong the efforts they engaged in,
Me those people will not see.

From the Dharma should one see the Buddha,
For the Dharma-bodies are the guides;
Yet Dharmahood is not something one should
become aware of,
Nor can one be made aware of it,

Put in another form:

Who sees me sees the Dhamma;
Who sees the Dhamma sees me.

The Buddha, the one who realized supreme Enlightenment is like a star. Subhuti asked: 'One speaks of Enlightenment. Of what is this a synonym?' The Lord said: 'Enlightenment is a synonym of Emptiness, of suchness (*tathatā*), of the Reality-limit, of the realm of Dharma.' Mañjuśri said: 'Enlightenment is not discerned by anyone, nor is it fully known, nor seen, nor heard, nor remembered. It is neither produced nor stopped, neither described nor expounded. In so far as there is any Enlightenment, that Enlightenment is neither existent nor non-existent, for there is nothing that could be fully known by Enlightenment, nor does Enlightenment fully know Enlightenment . . . "Non-existent are all *dharmas*"—that is a synonym of Enlightenment and it is thus that the realm of Dharma comes to be called thus. For, as the domain of the Buddha, all *dharmas* are non-separateness.'

Subhuti asked: 'How is Enlightenment attained?' The Lord said: 'Enlightenment is attained neither through a path nor through a no-path. Just the path is Enlightenment, just Enlightenment is the path.'

Subhuti asked: 'What then, is this supreme Enlightenment?' The Lord said: 'It is Suchness. Suchness neither grows nor diminishes. A *bodhisattva* who repeatedly and often dwells in mental activities connected with that Suchness, comes near to the supreme Enlightenment, and he does not lose those mental activities again. It is certain that there can be no growth or diminution of that which is beyond all words, and therefore neither the perfections, nor all *dharmas*, can grow or diminish. It is thus that, when he dwells in mental activities of this kind, a *bodhisattva* becomes one who is near to perfect enlightenment.'

Let us recall what was said at the beginning of this chapter: 'Apart from the mode of life of the *bodhisattvas*, there is nowhere any happiness for any being.' Who is a *bodhisattva*? He is a being who lives not for himself but is bound for full Enlightenment, his own and that of all others. 'So it is', said the Buddha, 'with a *bodhisattva* who is full of pity and concerned with the welfare of all beings, who dwells in friendliness, compassion, sympathetic joy and even-mindedness.' Wisdom and compassion are the most powerful motive forces in life. Great compassion characterises his relationship and conduct towards all sentient beings, and perfect wisdom his attitude to reality.

The Lord said: 'Doers of what is hard are the *Bodhisattvas* who have set out for the benefit and happiness of the world, out of pity for it. "We will become a shelter for the world, a refuge, the place of rest, the final relief, lights and leaders of the world. We will win full enlightenment and become the resort of the world"—with these words they make a vigorous effort to win full Enlightenment . . . Their meditation is prompted by the desire to fully know all *dharmas* . . . A *bodhisattva* is fearless in any situation, ready to cast away even his body, and to renounce all that is necessary to life . . . He produces an adamantine thought thus: "I should become one who never abandons all-beings. Towards all beings should I adopt the same attitude of mind. All beings I should lead to Nirvana. But even when I have led all beings to Nirvana, no being at all has been led to Nirvana. For one should look to the fact that all *dharmas* are neither produced nor stopped. Everywhere should I train myself to accomplish a penetration into all *dharmas*, to the consummation of the one principle of all *dharmas*, of the perfections, the Unlimited States, the *jhānas* and *samāpattis*, the super-knowledges, the ten powers, the grounds of self-confidence, the special *Buddha-dharmas*." Supported on this thought, the *bodhisattva* will cause innumerable beings to achieve the highest—and that without depending on anything. Moreover, the *bodhisattva* produces an adamantine thought thus: "For the sake of all suffering beings, I too will experience their sufferings until they have all become released in the realm of Nirvana which leaves nothing behind. Afterwards, I will fully awake to the utmost, right and perfect enlightenment" . . . As a saviour of all beings should a *bodhisattva* behave towards all beings.'

Wisdom and compassion are a unity, worked through the practice of the Six Perfections, the *pāramitās*; that is, methods for going to the Beyond. They are generosity, morality, patience, vigour, concentration, and the sixth, which is the master *pāramitā*, wisdom. The *bodhisattva* takes this great Vow.

> However innumerable sentient beings are, I vow to save them.
> However inexhaustible the defilements are, I vow to extinguish them.
> However immeasurable the *dharmas* are, I vow to master them.
> However incomparable enlightenment is, I vow to attain it.

Energized by this vow, the *bodhisattva* realizes the full fruition of the *pāramitās*. Like a star is the *bodhisattva*!

We have used the word 'Dharma' or *dharma* (Pali, Dhamma, *dhamma*). Derived from the root *dhr* (to hold or support), it is a word with many uses and meanings. Let us look at some:

(1a) Used as a proper name in Roman spelling with a capital *D*, it signifies a transcendental reality; Nirvana, for instance.
(1b) It can also signify the Buddha's Teachings.
(1c) It is the Moral Law.
(2a) As a common noun in italics with a small *d*, it can signify a law of the Universe; e.g. 'Hatred is never appeased by hatred; it can only be appeased by non-hatred. This is an everlasting *dharma*.'
(2b) It can signify a person's social or religious duty, or his/her vocation in life.

(2c) Within the Abhidhamma literature, which comprises the early philosophical systematizations of the Buddha's teachings, it has a special technical use. There it signifies a basic elemental event of sensory or mental experience, one that is ultimately real but momentary and discontinuous, existing only in series.*

The deep waters of the *Prajñāpāramitā* are very deep indeed. The Lord said: 'The Tathāgata has fully known all *dharmas* as not made. It is just through their essential nature that those *dharmas* are not a something. Their nature is no-nature and their no-nature is their nature, because all *dharmas* have one mark only, i.e., no-mark. For this reason all *dharmas* have the character of not having been fully known by the Tathāgata. For there are not two natures of *dharma*, but just one single one is the nature of all *dharmas*. And the nature of all *dharmas* is no-nature and their no-nature is their nature. It is thus that all points of attachment are abandoned.' Well might Subhuti exclaim, 'Hard to understand, O Lord, is the perfection of wisdom'; to which the Lord replied: 'Because nothing is fully known by the enlightened.'

Again, the Lord said: 'All *dharmas* are situated in space, they have not come, they have not gone, they are the same as space. Space has not come nor gone, it is not made, not unmade, not effected. It has not uprisen, it does not last, not endure. It is neither produced nor stopped. The same is true of all *dharmas* which are, after the fashion of space, non-discriminate, because the emptiness of form (and all other *dharmas*) neither comes nor goes, for all *dharmas* are situated in emptiness and from that situation they do not depart. They are situated in the signless, the wishless, the ineffective, in non-production, in no-birth, in the absence of positivity, in dream and self, in the boundless, in the calm quiet, in Nirvana, in the unrecoverable. They have not come nor gone, situated in immobility. They are situated in form (and in other

*For further elucidation see *The Central Conception of Buddhism and the Meaning of the Word 'Dharma'*, by Fyodor Stcherbatsky. Reprint, Delhi: Motilal Banarsidass, 1974. Ed.

skhandhas), and in the full enlightenment of Arhats and Pratyekabuddhas.'

Let us hear a few more statements from the *Prajñāpāramitā* for furthering the happy discomfiture of the logical, discursive, concept-making mind: 'In the ultimate sense there is neither karma nor karma-result, neither production nor stopping, neither defilement nor purification.' Mañjuśri said: '"Buddha", "self", "non-production", "the Trackless", are all synonymous terms . . . The Buddha is the same as speechless silence.' The Lord said: '"*Bodhisattva*", "perfect wisdom", "form", etc., are mere words, like magical illusions. They are not, do not arise, are false to behold . . . All that is conditioned is like flashing meteors, a fault of vision, a dream, a bubble.'

What, then, of the Unconditioned? Subhuti said: 'Like a dream, like a magical illusion are all beings, all *dharmas*, objective facts. So also is a fully enlightened Buddha, even Nirvana. And if perchance there could be anything more distinguished, of that too I would say that it is like an illusion, like a dream. For illusion and Nirvana are not two different things, nor are dreams and Nirvana.'

Such is the principal message of the *Prajñāpāramitā*—the unconditional identity of the conditioned and the Unconditioned.

The *Prajñāpāramitā* is concerned with the Absolute. What can one say about the Absolute? You can say whatever you think might reasonably be said about it, provided you will also cancel out each and every statement by saying the opposite. Any and every proposition as well as its opposite is affirmed and also denied. The result? The Void. The *śūnya*, the empty; or the *bindu*, the drop or no-thing which has no boundary, no dimensions. So, the non-finite, unconditioned non-depended, not-relative, Absolute. Do we thereby know the Absolute? No. The Absolute is the unknowable, for all knowing is caught within the net of the relative, the perishing.

What is the use, then, of the *Prajñāpāramitā*? The supreme use! For it can spell complete liberation from bondage to the known and the knowable.

How is this possible in view of what has been said so far? The liberation does not come just by making statements followed by negations of these statements.

Mere words are impotent. When the mind is utterly pure, empty, transparent, it is itself the truth, the living fact to which the words or thoughts are only pointers. This is liberation. It is simple, even as a perfect song beautifully sung is simple.

Buddhism and Yoga

(1973)

MAN'S PRIMORDIAL ANCESTOR, like all creation, lived in the state of communion, which is the state of yoga. Immortality, freedom and bliss were his, but he knew them not for his communion was a wholly unknowing one. As the ages passed, he felt the sting of self-consciousness making him say 'I am not you'. He felt the barb of desire making him serve his sense-lust and inject the poison of selfness into his whole life. His unknowing communion was a fool's paradise. Slowly but surely he was pushed out of it. And when the darkening shades of the knowledge of pleasure and pain ended, the timeless shining of that golden age of ignorant innocence, man's childhood, was over. He strayed away from his father's home, *Sukhāvat*, the home of harmless delight into the dark forest of lusty adolescence covered over with the terrors of hostile night.

Now no more could he meet his father or hear his voice. But there was the memory of him and of the bliss of being securely cradled in his everlasting arms. He could not call upon him by name for he had never known that name. And of his own name he knew only the sound and not the meaning. He knew not that the full meaning of his own name was also a name of his father, source and goal of all being.

This youth, lost in the dark forest, sought to know his true name. He sought to return to his eternal home. He sought his restoration to communion as the enlightened yogi.

Like an endless thread time spins out of eternity. Caught in the spin of time, which is *saṃsāra*, unenlightened man is in the ill-state, and is himself the producer of ill, whilst his parent, transcendent mind, wrapped in the folds of eternity, awaits in silence the home-coming of his beloved child. And the child is home when the light of wisdom envelops his whole being. For then he is full-grown Man, like his father whose body is truth itself, the *Dharmakāya*. Mind and Man are now one in the communion of the enlightened state.

This homeward journey is yoga. The first step in this journey is bodily ablution. The body is the living psycho-physical organism, *nāma-rūpa*; that is, manifested shape and its informing principle; or the five *skandhās*—shape, feelings, percepts, mental patterns, and discriminative consciousness. This is a man's body. The ablution is effected by the water of purity: purity of thought and feeling, of speech and deed. This ablution is not merely a skin wash, for the water of purity goes through and through till the whole body is purity itself. Later, this water will change into fire and then into light, for such is yoga.

The *Śāṇḍilya Upanishad* (1.4–14) gives us the nature of the water of purity: 'In thought, word and deed let there be harmlessness, truthfulness, non-covetousness, continence, kindliness, equanimity; patience, endurance, steadiness of mind in gain or loss, abstemiousness in eating and drinking, and cleanliness of body and mind; and also austerity, contentment with what comes naturally, charity and so on.' The Buddha and Śāriputta (*M.I.*, 15/16 and 36/37) teach that we must be rid of the following defilements of mind: greed, ill-will and covetousness, anger, malevolence, hypocrisy, spite, envy, stinginess, deceit, treachery, obstinacy, impetuosity, arrogance, pride, conceit, indolence.

This purification is the indispensable foundation for yoga. Side by side with this go bodily discipline and meditation in the full sense of these terms. Clearly then, yoga is no other than the complete ending of all *dukkha* through living the holy life in its fullness in the world. It is also clear that the approach to yoga must be pure, free of selfness, devoid of all delusions that I will achieve or attain or gain anything whatsoever. There is nothing for me; and indeed there cannot be anything for me, for I am *no-thing*.

Provided moral purity is present, the discipline of abstemiousness in food and drink, of rest and activity, of the right use of the senses, and of postures (*āsana*) and breathing (*prāṇāyāma*), becomes meaningful. The Buddha taught his disciples to partake of one meal only each day and that before noon. We read in the *Sekha* and *Brahmāyu Suttas* that in the *bhikkhu*'s discipline, 'food is not for fun or indulgence or personal charm or beautification, but just enough for the support of his body and keeping it going, for keeping it unharmed and for furthering the holy life' (*M.1.* 355 and *M.2* 138). And of the Buddha himself we read that, 'when he has eaten he sits silent for a moment, but he does not let pass the time for giving thanks. When he has eaten he gives thanks' (*M.2.* 139).

The *Yogatattva Upanishad* (verse 28) presents harmlessness and scanty eating as the most important religious observance and self-restraint, and the *Amṛitañada* (verse 27) states that excessive eating is an obstacle to yoga.

To appreciate the significance of such teachings, let us note that the first expression of greed in our life is for food, and of rage when denied food or frustrated from eating more. Again, one of the main transgressions of the first moral precept (*śīla*) of which the world is guilty is the slaying of living creatures for food. Remember that harmlessness in thought, word and deed is a main root of holiness. The Buddha said, 'He who lives neither tormenting himself nor tormenting others lives with a self become Brahman' (*M.1.* 341–9, and 412–13).

Associated with right conduct and care of the body are the postures and breathing. If we practise them in order to slim or to gratify vanity, to gain health or success or power over others; in short for any worldly or self-centred motive, the penalty will have to be suffered sooner or later. Physical well-being and other good things may appear as incidentals, but they are obstacles to yoga if they are objects of gratification of desire.

If the postures and breathing are practised in the right spirit, there will be a cessation of all squandering of energy, especially in the form of all noisy chatter. What a blessing! For then only can there be human conversation, or a true communion.

It is easy to fall into the trap of thinking of posture and breathing exclusively in physical terms. Listen, then, to some of the supreme yogis of the past. As regards posture, Yājñvalkya, the prince of yogis, is taught by the Lord Sūrya Nārāyaṇa that, 'Being firm in unshaken wisdom constitutes posture' (*Maṇḍalabrāhmāṇa Upanishad*, 2.2.5.) In the *Tejobindu Upanishad* (1.25) we read: 'That should be known as posture in which one can meditate uninterruptedly on Brahman, with ease and without fatigue.' As regards breathing, the *Tejobindu* says (1.31): 'That is called breath-restraint (*prāṇāyāma*) in which there is the control of the modifications of the mind through the cognition of Brahman in all states of consciousness. The avoidance of being impressed by the phenomenal world is said to be expiration (*recaka*). The awareness "I am Brahman only" is inspiration (*pūraka*). The constant retention of this awareness without any agitation is the retention or cessation of the breath (*kumbhaka*). The ignorant merely close their nostrils, or, suffer from nose-ache.' And in the *Varāha Upanishad* (5. 56–58) we read: 'Taking his stand on himself when Brahman is seen, rejecting everything caused by ignorance of the Ātman is expiration. Absorbing the wisdom of the scriptures is inspiration and keeping oneself in the knowledge of Brahman is retention of the breath.'

The Buddhist who bears the above in mind when practising *ānāpāna sati*, mindfulness in breathing as taught by the Buddha to Rāhula (*M.1.* 425) and also to a great assembly of monks (*M.3.* 82–84), will find great benefit, for it establishes your individual rhythm of existence, and the life-process flows along in peace. We must understand clearly that the postures and breathing are a means for reducing to a minimum the obstructiveness of the psycho-physical organism to meditation, *samādhi*.

The yogically disciplined, that is, the religiously prepared body, is a living *maṇḍala*, or an animate expression as a finite human form of the immeasurable creative energy of pure mind. See the deep meaning of this and we can understand the statement in the *Maitreya Upanishad* (2.1.2.) that 'the body is said to be a temple. That which lives in it is Śhiva (the Ever Auspicious)'; and the words of

Paul in his first epistle to the Corinthians (6.19), 'Know ye not that your body is the temple of the Holy Spirit in you, which ye have of God, and ye are not your own?' You, the living *maṇḍala*, are the form divine in miniature. You are the microcosm which represents the universal form divine, the macrocosm. It is your divine destiny to be the living vehicle of transcendence, if you really care. If I really care, I release the skill to absent myself. Thereupon yoga is realized through me. Such is the mystery. However that is realized, that way of realization is yoga.

Let us now try to understand some of the teachings which are the basis of yoga, noting also a few differences between Hindu and Buddhist presentations.

Ancient Indian tradition presents two fundamental properties of the universe: (1) **Motion**, and (2) that in which it takes place, namely **Space**. (Since our English words are not wholly adequate for our purpose, let us use a few Sanskrit words also.) *Ākāśa*, or space, is that through which all things possess finite extension or body; that is, through which they make an appearance. In addition to space as we ordinarily sense it, *ākāśa* is also mind-space, or *cittākāśa*, in which the discriminative activity of consciousness functions; and also, in the context of pure awareness in which there is no subject-object duality, it is *cidākāśa*.

What we call material things are the gross form of *ākāśa* itself, space concretized, so to say. In its subtle forms it merges into forms of energy such as heat or light. This *ākāśa* is measurable—it can be controlled and used by us. In contrast, *ākāśa* which is mind, space is non-finite, im-measurable. There is no specific *here* or *there* in it.

The principle of motion is *prāṇa*, which is life-energy, the rhythm of the universe. I am using the word 'life' in the old sense, its total sense, not in the restricted biological sense in which we use it nowadays. All the dynamic forces of the universe, objective, mental or spiritual, are modifications of *prāṇa*. Breathing, so indispensable to the life of the body, is only one of many functions through which *prāṇa*, which is life in its most extensive meaning, manifests itself. *Prāṇa* is more than breath, nervous energy, the creative power of semen, the faculties of thought and intellect or of will-power, all of which are expressions of *prāṇa*. The centres of psychocosmic force in the human body (*cakras*) and their respective organs correspond to the modifications of *ākāśa* and through these *prāṇa* flows and operates. Thus we see that what is called *prāṇāyāma* in yoga is very much more than a technique of physical breathing.

It is important to bear in mind that whilst it is convenient and even necessary to talk of *prāṇa* and *ākāśa* separately, they cannot be separated in the supreme sense. They are one, whole non-duality. Regard *prāṇa* as the father, *ākāśa* as the mother. And in this connection recall the Mosaic commandment: 'Honour thy father and mother that thy days may be long upon the land which the Lord thy God giveth thee' (Exodus 20.12). *Prāṇa* the father and *ākāśa* the mother are a non-duality because they are in timeless conjugation.

The practical teaching of yoga is presented as the control and directing of *prāṇa* through a series of psychic centres, the *cakras*, by way of a system of **physical** channels, the *nāḍīs*. The *cakras* and *nāḍīs* are associated, spatially, with different positions in the spine and with various nerves. They should *not*, however, be regarded as identical with the physical organs, although there is some relationship with them, since we know that mental activities, especially in meditation, do produce physical results.

Let us now briefly consider the *cakras*. We start at the base of the spine with the first *cakra*, the *mūladhāra*, which means 'root support'. It represents—remember it only *represents*—the element Earth. The *Muṇḍaka Upanishad* says (2.1.4.): 'Earth is the footing of the Lord'. In Isaiah (66.1) and in the Acts of the Apostles (7.49) you find 'Heaven is my Throne, and Earth my Footstool.' The authors of those words were practical yogis who expressed their own realization in beautiful symbolic language.

Mūlādhāra contains the unqualified primordial energy, which serves either the functions of physical reproduction and rejuvenation or transmutes these forces into spiritual potentialities. We must distinguish the working of this psychical energy from that of the electrical and chemical energy in physiological processes that take place in the body. The energy of *mūlādhāra* is the psychical counterpart of physiological energy. The latent energy of this centre is called *kuṇḍalinī śakti*. *Kuṇḍalinī* is the name of the goddess who is said to preside over all power. The female aspect—the negative aspect—of the whole universe, including man, is the active aspect: the aspect of power in operation. The male aspect has a different kind of dynamism altogether. It is a dynamism which functions in perfect stillness, which is a dynamic, not static, poise. Now the effects of *kuṇḍalinī śakti* can be either divine or demoniac. The impure man is destroyed. Only the one who is pure in mind and heart and lives a simple, austere life can utilize *kuṇḍalinī śakti* and handle it safely. It is said to sleep coiled up like a serpent at the base of the spine. Like a serpent! You know how Moses and Aaron went to Pharaoh. Aaron cast his rod and it became a serpent. Then Pharaoh called his magicians, who cast their rods, which also turned into serpents. But Aaron's rod swallowed up all those rods (Exodus 7. 10–12). Unawakened, *kuṇḍalinī* is absorbed into subconscious and bodily functions. Released, it finds perfect unfoldment and final realization in the seventh *cakra*, which is known as the *sahasrāra*, the thousand-petalled lotus, which corresponds to the brain itself, the cerebrum.

The second *cakra*, situated in the genital region, is *svādhiṣṭhāna*, which means 'own abode'. And it is called 'own abode' because, as far as the living body as an animal body, and our sense of separate selfhood are concerned, the most intense ego assertion is expressed through procreative activity. *Svādhiṣṭhana* represents the element water. In Buddhist yoga we have a slight difference. Buddhist yoga tends to group *mūlādhāra* and *svādhiṣṭhāna* together as a single root centre, as a sacral plexus, not separate pelvic and hypogastric plexuses.

The third *cakra* is called *maṇipūra*, which means 'lustrous as a gem'. It represents the element fire, and is concerned with the forces of physical and psychical transformation of all the commerce of the daily living process. It is usually associated with the navel. Sometimes it is called the *nābhipadma*—the 'navel lotus.' There is a profound significance to the navel. The umbilical cord connects the infant before its birth from the navel to the mother. Through the navel every one of us in the world is connected right up to our remotest ancestry.

The fourth *cakra* is called *anāhata*. Here we come to something very significant. *Anāhata* means 'the place where the *munis* hear the sound which comes without striking two things together'. The *muni* is the holy one who is the silent one. He speaks only when necessary, and only what is necessary. But that is merely the outward physical aspect, for with a little practice, some of us could quite well appear to be *munis*! There is therefore a profound inward aspect too. The *muni*'s silence is the silence of the mind. It means the end of that incessant chatter that goes on in the brain day and night. The *muni* is silent in that sense far more than in the physical sense. *Anāhata* is the place where the *muni* hears the sound which comes without striking two things together: he hears the sound of the pulse of life, of *prāṇa*. Whilst still an embryo, perhaps the first thing one becomes aware of inside the mother's body is the sound of the beating of the mother's heart; and perhaps also of that peculiar roaring sound which you hear too if you dive into water, the sound of the circulation of the mother's blood. These physical sounds we can describe, but the sound of the pulse of life is indescribable. You must experience it for yourself. It has no relationship to physical sound as we know it and as investigated by science. For physical sound reaches us through physical media: air; any gaseous medium; any liquid medium; any solid medium. It does not travel through a vacuum though. But this sound which the *munis* hear is the sound whose source, they declare, is *ākāśa* as 'ether', not *ākāśa* as solid, liquid, or gas. I am using the word 'ether', which we used up to the end of the last century, purely for convenience as there is no precise modern English equivalent. So, too, one uses the word 'hear', but obviously one doesn't hear with the physical ears in the usual way; this is another kind of hearing. *Anāhata* represents the element air, but one may wonder whether this means air in the sense in which we use the word today—a mixture of gases—or whether it means what we used to know as ether. *Anāhata* is concerned with respiration, and it is situated on the vertical, central axis of the body, at the level of the heart.

The fifth *cakra*, called *viśuddhi*, which means 'made pure', is the throat centre. It is concerned with speech and with mantric sound; that is, the use of the voice to produce deep, psychical effects. We must not understand speech here in the ordinary sense. The speech with which the yogis were concerned, as far as the *viśuddhi cakra* was concerned, was prophetic speech. He who could take *kuṇḍalinī* safely up to the *viśuddhi cakra* was in tune with the realm of Transcendence. The words he uttered and any gesture he made, somehow inspired the listener and aroused a sense of Transcendence in him. So the *viśuddhi cakra*, as far as its mantric effect is concerned, must be regarded as the source of the word of power. It represents *ākāśa* as ether.

Next we come to the *ājñā cakra*, associated with the *medulla*, so called because the 'command of the teacher is Received from above'. That is the symbolic language in which it is put. Some may prefer to put it this way: it is heard from within, because you yourself are both teacher and learner. What you receive from someone else stimulates you. If the stimulus is of the right sort, then that which enlightens you is within yourself. If you are quiet and alert and sensitive, you learn, and you learn the deep things that are beyond words, beyond concepts, and free of all the limitations of discursive thinking. That is what *ajñā* deals with. It represents insight into the truth which is Transcendence.

Finally, the *sahasrāra*, the crown centre, or the 'thousand-petalled lotus', as it is called. It represents the infinite variety and sum-total of all that is represented by all the six *cakras*, but is regarded as of a higher order altogether. It is as if a new octave of being and consciousness begins with *sahasrāra*. It is the abode of *Śiva Sadāśiva*. *Śiva* (Shiva) is the name of the third person of the Hindu trinity; it means, 'The Auspicious One'. *Sadāśiva* means 'The Ever Auspicious One'. This *cakra* is therefore the abode of the supreme deity within your own being. The transition from *ajñā* to *sahasrāra* represents the liberation out of all separate selfhood into Transcendence. One is no longer in charge of oneself, which means that the separate self-consciousness is no longer in charge of one's total being, because Transcendence itself has taken over.

In Christian terminology, 'the manhood is taken up into the Godhead'.

Since *ajñā* and *sahasrāra* are so close to each other, they are sometimes, as in Buddhist yoga, regarded as a single crown centre. The word *cakra* means 'wheel'; the crown and throat centres are the front wheels, and the heart and navel centres are the rear wheels, of the fiery chariot of the spirit in its ascent to Transcendence. Think of Elijah being taken up to Heaven in the fiery chariot.

Now a few words about the *nāḍīs* or channels. *Prāṇa* reveals itself in the form of two dynamic tendencies. The polar currents of force which flow in the body are (1) the *solar* energies, through the *piṇgalā nāḍī*, which is on the right side of the vertebral column, representing the forces of the day; that is, centrifugal forces which tend towards conscious awareness, objective knowledge, differentiation, intellectual discrimination; and (2) the *lunar* energies, through the *īḍā nāḍī* which is on the left side of the vertebral column, symbolizing the forces of the night, working in the darkness of the subconscious mind. They are the undifferentiated, regenerative, centripetal forces, flowing from the all-encompassing source of life and tending towards re-unification, for example, in the impulses of love, of all that had been separated by the intellect.

The most important channel is the *suṣumṇā nāḍī*, which runs like a hollow channel through the centre of the spinal column, meeting *īḍā* and *piṇgalā* in the perineum at the base of the spine. The *suṣumṇā* is able to cause a synthesis not only of the solar and lunar currents, which are forms of *prāṇa*, but also of the seven centres vertically, upwards from the base of the spine to the brain. This integration is experienced successively through the *cakras*. The *suṣumṇā* is a symbol of all the potentialities which lie dormant in every human being, and which can be realized by the yogi. One such potentiality is the faculty of becoming directly conscious of the inner relationship between ideas, things, facts, sense data, and forces.

Now in, the usual cross-legged postures which we learn and practise in yoga, *mūlādhāra* is in touch with Mother Earth. So here we have the contact of earth to Earth, since *mūlādhāra* represents earth, and the microcosm is in sensitive relationship with the macrocosm. Similarly, Mother Earth in relation to Space is a microcosm sensitively related to the supreme macrocosm. Thus all the psychic energies which emanate out of that which we in the ordinary way call matter, and the psychic energies which are concerned with man, the living person, are in right relationship—earth to Earth.

The spinal column is called *merudaṇḍa*. *Daṇḍa* means 'stick', or 'rod', and in this case it happens to be a living rod. *Mount Meru* is the sacred mountain or *axis mundi* of classical Hindu cosmology, the place where the ultimate realization takes place. So this *daṇḍa* leads right up to the top of the *Mount Meru* of the microcosm, the individual, which is the point at which Transcendence itself makes contact with the living person. In the cross-legged posture *merundaṇḍa* is upright, like a lightning conductor, and *sahasrāra*, the topmost *cakra*, points to the celestial zenith. So, earth to earth, and also, just as Mother Earth is related to the celestial zenith, so is the yogi related through *sahasrāra* to the celestial zenith. The energy (*prāṇa*) of matter radiates out macroscopically from earth to cosmos, and in the yogi, up microscopically from *mūlādhāra* to *sahasrāra*. If you are well prepared, the energy of Transcendence responds through *sahasrāra* down to *mūlādhāra*, sensitizing, refining, and transforming you. That is why, if you sit properly, at ease, elastic, still and silent, you experience all the extraordinary benefit that comes out of such practice. But never forget the indispensable preliminary: the purity of the mind and the heart, and of daily life. When this is accomplished, the finite you is fully subsumed in the Infinite. The wound of separation between man and mind is healed. Once again, there is the primordial unity. Benediction floods your being, and spreads through you all over Earth. *Merudaṇḍa*, whilst you are still caught fast in worldliness, is the tree of good and evil. *Merudaṇḍa*, after the complete reversal of worldliness, and consequent restoration of life to a state of holiness, is the Tree of Life.

Let us briefly consider a few points in connection with the transformation of consciousness, which is the fundamental objective of the yogi. When *kuṇḍalinī śakti* is awakened in the purified individual by means of secret meditation and physical techniques, it is led upwards from *mūlādhāra* to *sahasrāra*, step by step through all the *cakras*. Each of these stages marks a transformation of consciousness. As you go upward and emerge into a profounder state of consciousness, the old is not destroyed or annihilated but all its essence is taken up into the new state. There is no annihilation whatsoever. The ascent spans the entire range from worldly consciousness to Transcendence itself.

The human body is an animal body. As such, it is much concerned with the preservation of itself and of the species. Hence food and sex play dominant parts in human life. Thus the three lower *cakras*, *mūlādhāra*, *svādhiṣṭthāna*, and *maṇipūra*, are largely involved with our mundane life. Then we come to *anāhata*, the heart centre, where true egohood is realized. True egohood means that one is self-responsibly self-conscious, devoid of egoism and free of the tyranny of desire. Such true egohood contains within itself the energy for transcending itself. The transcending will take place very consciously, and only from within yourself. Nature cannot go any further without your deliberate co-operation. You have the power to say *Yes* or *No*. You must care, and if you really care, man comes to fulfilment and fruition through each and every one of us. There is no such thing as fruition or fulfilment for any man in isolation.

In *anāhata*, the pacification of the sense consciousness takes place, and one enters the first deep state of meditation. Real meditation begins there. If you examine the process that goes on in your mind throughout the day, you will find that sense impressions and sense images keep rising up after they have sunk into the sub-conscious and clamour for attention. The mind is a jungle, a confusion. You have to find your own way out of it. Watch it. Follow it. Don't fight against it, don't give way to it, don't indulge it. That is your task—a tricky one, a difficult one. But when you do it, the clamour of the sense-consciousnesses will subside, and for the first time you will know the meaning of peace. It is not the mere opposite of turmoil and strain, but that which transcends the conflict of the dualities, of quiet and turmoil.

The next is the *viśuddhi cakra*. Here one goes quite beyond the word, which means beyond finitude and mortality. Here, in the realm of prophetic speech, is the second deep stage of meditation where all discursive thinking as such comes to an end. Certain thoughts will still rise up, but they will flow along calmly, for all self-association with them as well as their origination through one's own desire have ceased. This is the great significance of the *viśuddhi cakra* as such. Here unified mind—made one: whole for the first time—functions at its own level and in its own right. Its receptive-responsive sensitivity is at its peak and there is the release from isolative self-consciousness. At the *ajñā cakra* one goes beyond all ideation. There is direct perception of the great archetypes.

Lastly, in *sahasrāra* there is complete pacification of all sense consciousness, freedom from isolative self-consciousness and self-obtrusion upon Totality. We as we are obtrude upon the world, but in full *samādhi* that obtrusiveness completely ceases and there is no conflict between self and not-self. You realize holiness, blissfully and ineffably. In that state there is nothing that one may call 'my' mind, because one has become empty, transparent, whereupon that which is commonly spoken of as the divine mind or the cosmic mind functions freely through you. In this state, power can be handled safely, for now love and wisdom are in perfect harmony, whereas in the ordinary worldly state we always mishandle power.

In the upward ascent from *mūlādhāra*, *kuṇḍalinī ṣakti* releases herself out of the sphere of duality and conflict. At *anāhata* begins the first rapport with Transcendence, culminating in *sahasrāra*, the abode of *Śiva*—peaceful, auspicious, non-moving but universally active, infinite and immeasurable. And there *Śakti* enjoys the bliss of union with her Lord, *Śiva*. Father and mother are one. It is in this state that one realizes the meaning of the words of Jesus after he had ascended: 'All power is given unto Me in Heaven and Earth.'

The united *Śiva-Śakti* returns to *mūlādhāra*, as they say in the books. It not only returns to *mūlādhāra*: the united *Śiva-Śakti* rises up again and makes its final abode, during the lifetime of the yogi, at *anāhata*, because it is at this level that one is in tune with all mankind. What happens? The united *Śiva-Śakti,* coming right down to *mūlādhāra,* completely purifies, refines and sensitizes the whole being. You are the perfected holy one. But if you just remain there you are isolated. As the united *Śiva-Śakti* ascends again to *anāhata* it transcendentalizes all the worldly functions represented by *mulādhāra, svādhiṣṭhāna* and *manipūra,* and the work which falls to our lot in ordinary, everyday life; and it enables you to be in sensitive psychical touch with any being. *Śiva-Śakti* resides at *anāhata* in the perfected holy one until the time of death, when it rises up to *sahasrāra* again and the end of the body takes place.

From *mūlādhāra* to *sahasrāra* is from earth to heaven. The *Maitreya* and the *Skanda Upanishads* say: 'The Body (of the Purified One) is the Temple of the Lord.' The dweller in that temple is *Śiva* himself. Or in the words of Isaiah: 'The heaven is my throne, and the earth is my footstool; what manner of house will ye build unto me? And what place shall be my rest?' To which the yogi answers: 'This pure body shall be thy House of Life, O Lord. Thy place of rest shall be *Anāhata* whilst this body lives; and in its dying, thou shalt enter thy own Sabbath through the portal of *Sahasrāra*.'

And so the young man, who strayed far from his father and was lost in a dark forest, rediscovers his true name and is reunited in communion as a buddha, a fully enlightened one.

Buddhahood

(1977)

WE WILL NOW consider that which is free of all measure, change, limitation. But how shall we talk of the non-descript and non-finite, the signless and unconditioned?

Sense, speech and thought obstruct the functioning of the transcendent dimension of Mind. So we are fragmented and scattered about, and we cannot *be*. With senses pacified and speech and thought vibrantly still, we can *be*, and also *un-be*. Then mind in its fullness wholly subsumes sense, speech and thought, which thereupon unlock the gates of the impossible.

•

What does the Buddha say of himself? Answering Upaka, he declares[1] he is victorious over all evil, free of craving, all awakened, a supreme teacher, perfected, one who has realized Nirvana. Addressing the five *bhikkhus* at Isipatana, the Tathāgata announces that the Deathless is found; he teaches the Dharma; if they lived in accord with it they would realize the supreme goal of the holy life, the Deathless, Nirvana, and unshakable freedom of mind.[2] He assures Ganaka Moggallāna:[3] 'Nirvana exists, the way leading to Nirvana exists, and I exist as adviser . . . A Shower of the Way is the Tathāgata.'

Without purity, the mind is ill-conditioned, in *dukkha*, and cannot see truth. Whenever we say that we perceive something, we are in fact perceiving our own mental construct brought into being by the stimulus with which that external or internal something provided us, not truth, and we remain unenlightened.

Hui Neng says:[4] 'Those who wish to hear the teaching should first purify their own mind, and after hearing it they should each clear up their own doubts in the same way as the sages did in the past.' Again: 'When one is free from defilements, wisdom reveals itself and will not be separated from the essence of mind.' And again: 'The slow-witted fail to enlighten themselves when the Dharma is made known to them, because they are thickly veiled by erroneous views and deeply-rooted defilements.' Hui Neng then proceeds to talk of perfection: 'Erroneous views keep us in defilement, while right views remove us from it. But when we are in a position to discard both of them, then we are absolutely pure.' This is precisely what Gotama taught in the Parable of the Raft.[5]

Let there be no illusions regarding the teaching of going beyond virtue and vice. Release from the virtue-vice duality means that, freed of vice, you are *virtue* embodied. An enlightened one, a buddha, is never guilty of unvirtuous conduct in act or speech or thought on any account.

In *The Opening of the Wisdom Eye*,* H.H. the Dalai Lama says (p. 87): 'The person who wants to practise the way of tantric instruction should observe well all the precepts for *it is only on the basis of virtuous conduct,* sila, *that one can advance along the Path.'*

The seal of confirmation of all this comes from the Buddha himself, when he says[6] to the dying Vakkali, 'He who sees the *Dhamma* sees me; he who sees me sees the *Dhamma.'* Thus in his own person as Śakyamuni, the Nirmānakāya, he is the embodied Transcendence. Unobstructed Transcendence, namely Tathāgata, functioning freely through Siddhattha Gotama, is declared to be 'deep, unfathomable, trackless'. For Tathāgata, there is no arising, no proceeding, no subsiding. Continuity, and space and time, do not apply here, nor do differentiation and containment as an entity within a space-time continuum. So there are no signs of being, no marks, no characteristics. Measureless, *Dhamma*-become, *Brahma*-become, is the Tathāgata: emptiness, *śūnyatā*, suchness, *tathatā*,

*Bangkok: Social Science Association of Thailand, 1968.

which is pure mind. So when Huang Po was asked[7] 'What is the Buddha?', he answered, 'Mind is the Buddha, while the cessation of conceptual thought is the Way.'

This cessation of conceptual thought is repeatedly presented by the Buddha in terms of the *jhānas* and the *samāpattis*. It is realized, not by suppressing thought by mental tricks or by anaesthetizing the mind, but by letting it become utterly pacified through perfect mindfulness, the indispensable basis of moral habit. Virtue is the healthy, resilient backbone of the living Buddha. If trashy trinkets fill that jewel-casket, your own existential being, where could you put the pearl beyond price bestowed upon you?

To understand these statements, first consider some remarks in *The Diamond Sūtra*. The Lord said (chap. 4): 'Subhuti, when a Bodhisattva gives gifts he should not be supported by sight-objects, nor by sounds, smells, tastes, touchables, or by mind-objects. For, Subhuti, the Bodhisattva should give gifts in such a way that he is not supported by the notion of a sign.' Sign, *nimitta*, is a technical term for an object of sense. Ordinarily, we take the data of everyday existence as signs of realities. But in truth, sense-objects are empty. The Absolute is signless. It is not perceivable, still less recognizable, when it takes us up into itself. It takes us up into itself when we are devoid of our obstructive perceptions, our notions of signs. Such notions are misperceptions—mental defilements of which we are emptied when, passing beyond the *samāpatti* spoken of as the abiding in the condition of neither perception nor non-perception, there is the cessation of all perception and feeling. All conceptual thought has ended—not only the flow of conceptual thought, but also the latent seeds which sprout as concepts, as seminal concepts at first—the creative Word or Logos spoken of in various scriptures—and afterwards as the concepts which are the basic material and structuring agents of the flow of discursive thought of everyday experience.

In this cessation, it is not we as self-conscious individuals who abide in it. It is the Absolute, Transcendence, the Buddha, that now abides in us finite mortals. It is Buddhahood, pure mind, realizing its ineffable reality through us, mere signs certainly, but signs whose purity and perfection offer no resistance to that Suchness, that Voidness. When that happens, you the *Bodhisattva can* produce a true perception, and the 'thirty-two marks of the Buddha'—which are no marks!—are yours.

How can one *let* this come about? Gotama the Buddha put it thus: Cease from all grasping. In the practice of perfect mindfulness, observe intently the entire becoming-process, remaining free of self-association with it in terms of either attachment or aversion. Be clearly aware that every *rūpa, vedanā, saññā, sankhāra* and *viññāna* is *anicca,* impermanent, relative, an ephemeral spatio-temporal existent only: nothing to be attached to, not a cause for giving rise to aversion. Observe dispassionately and let the stream of the becoming-process flow on without grasping at any element whatsoever, bearing well in mind that attachment and aversion are both forms of grasping and of being grasped. In the absence of attachment and aversion, there is the absence of separate selfhood. Then there can be no grasping. The Lord tells[8] Ananda: 'A *bhikkhu* who has grasping does not attain final Nirvana . . . *(but)* a *bhikkhu* who is without grasping, O Ananda, does attain final Nirvana . . . *(and again)* This is deathlessness, that is to say the deliverance of thought without grasping.'

In the Greater Discourse to Saccaka, a Jain who is addressed by his clan name, Aggivessana, the Buddha says:[9] 'Now I, Aggivessana, am aware that when I am teaching *Dhamma* to companies consisting of many hundreds, each person thinks thus about me: "The recluse Gotama is teaching *Dhamma* especially for me." But this, Aggivessana, should not be understood thus. For when a Tathāgata is teaching *Dhamma* to others it is for the sake of general instruction. And I, Aggivessana, at the close of such a talk, steady, calm, make one-pointed and concentrate my mind subjectively in that first characteristic of concentration (*samādhi*) in which I ever constantly abide.'

This first characteristic of concentration in which the Tathāgata ever constantly abides, as the commentary[10] explains, is the *śūññataphalasamādhi,* that is, the concentration, or silent collectedness, on the fruit of voidness. Buddhahood is thus marked by a constant abiding in

Transcendence. When the living Buddha converses or walks or eats or sleeps, this abiding in Transcendence expresses itself extrovertedly: and in this connection it is most interesting and significant that the Buddha's behaviour and manners are faultless. When he teaches, or enters into meditation, the abiding in Transcendence expresses itself in an inward activity, a non-activity in the worldly sense, which is a well-spring of benediction and healing, for such meditation or teaching is an inspiring and a quickening energy functioning from a transcendent depth.

Consonant with the above is his affirmation[11] that he is without attachment or aversion or confusion. Even in sleep he is perfectly mindful[12] and remains free of all confusion. Thus Buddhahood means that an enlightened one is free of dreams in his sleep, of fantasies during the day and of any trace of disorder in mind. He is free of all the *āsavā*, the overflows of consciousness into pleasure-lust, into becoming such and such, into speculation, into ignorance.

Hence the Buddha is one who is not liable to delusion, and he claims that he possesses the *deva*-vision and the *deva*-hearing which enable him to see and hear far more sensitively and intimately than ordinary people do. What is far more important is that he knows by his own mind the mind and nature of others; which means that when he meets you, he can see and know the whole of you exactly as you are. In the words of Kaccāna the Great, he knows what should be known about you and sees what should be seen in you. So he knows just what is right and useful for you at your stage and gives you the teaching which will tame you and train you. The organism is tamed, the mind is trained. Thus the Lord is the incomparable charioteer of men to be tamed, he is the bringer to the goal, *attha*, that is, to the meaning or significance of the matter in hand.

Kaccāna the Great also said that the Lord is the giver of the Deathless. How does the Lord give the Deathless? By showing the Way. Here prime place is given to non-grasping and to putting aside with right wisdom all that is *annica* or relative, *anattā* or not ultimate reality, *dukkha* or far from the Absolute, from the self-existent unoriginated Nirvana. In other words, to put aside all that is finite, substanceless, mortal. And this teaching causes perplexity, for how do we put aside the entire manifested universe?

Consider carefully and calmly. In what does finitude or mortality subsist? Is plurality or is unity the fact? Now, are not words like 'finitude' or 'mortality' indicators of the mode in which we are conscious of reality, the mode of *viññāna* or discriminative consciousness? And does not this *viññāna* function as an isolative self-consciousness and as a separative object-consciousness, thus splitting up the unitary wholeness or Holiness of the Absolute into innumerable fragments? Does not this splitting up make us see the ageless, immortal life and the one total reality as countless separate objects and as many births and deaths, and feel it as pain and sorrow? And because we are blind to the complete inter-relatedness of the infinite variety within the single whole—the mysterious paradox that the one is the many and the many integrally constitute the one—are we not imprisoned by ignorance, *avidyā*, fast-fettered by greed and hate and delusion, by fear and violence?

If we can understand the above, we shall see that liberation or Nirvana consists in the transmutation of our present mortal mode of discriminative consciousness into the immortal mode of whole awareness. *Viññāna* changes into what the Buddha called *viññānaṃ anidassanaṃ anantaṃ sabbato pabhaṃ*,[13] that is, *viññāna* which is no longer merely discriminative but which is uncharacterized or infinite, endless or deathless, shining in every respect. Such is *Tathāgata*; such is the meaning of 'Gone Thus'.

What now is the meaning of 'putting aside with right wisdom?' What is the instrument for putting aside? The instrument is death: a constant dying by non-grasping, by letting go of everything that uprises in the becoming-process, *saṃsāra*, in every passing moment of time whilst you are alive bodily. Thus you live free in the eternal *now*, and not constricted in time and by time's sorrow. Death is the spiritual means by which the realization by Totality, of its own eternity and transcendence through an unobstructing you, the temporal being, takes place. It is not you the finite mortal who becomes a Tathāgata. It is Tathāgata-ness, Buddhahood, which is fruitively active in and through you, a *vajrasattva*, a diamond soul. This fruitive action is the pulse of creation, made manifest in the world as production-transformation through *your* non-grasping and *your* freedom from attachment and aversion, and *your* mastery of death. The transformative aspect is the meaning of death as the instrument, the spiritual means of putting aside with right wisdom. This use of death is the full, profound meaning of *nirodha*, commonly translated as 'extinction' or 'fading away'. When you die thus in every momentary creative pulse, your mastery of death releases the Deathless. In this sense the Tathāgata is the giver of the Deathless.

[1] M.I.171/2.
[2] M.I.205.
[3] M.III.6.
[4] *The Sutra of Hui Neng*, pp. 29, 34, 36—tr. Wong Mou-Lam, ed. Christmas Humphreys. Shanghai, 1930; London, 1940 (revised edition).
[5] M.I.135, 260, 455/6.
[6] Samyutta, III. 120.
[7] *The Zen Teaching of Huang Po*, p. 67—tr. John Blofeld. London, 1947.
[8] M.II.265.
[9] M.I.249.
[10] M.A.II.292.
[11] M.I.237
[12] M.I.249.
[13] M.I.329.

The Good Friend

An Eightieth Birthday Appreciation of Christmas Humphreys

(1981)

THE NAMES of all who are born are written in the *ākāśic* records. Only a few of these names are not erased at death.

Eighty years ago, shortly after noon on 15 February, Zoë Marguerite Humphreys presented her husband, Travers Humphreys, with a second son. Today, the world knows that son as Christmas Humphreys.* To some who enjoy the privilege of his friendship he is 'Toby', and as Toby I have known him for over thirty years. Prior to that we were contemporaries at Cambridge; he was 'Humphreys' and I was 'Mehta', the use of surnames being the customary mode of address amongst undergraduates unless intimate friendship or family relationship warranted the familiarity of personal names.

Two forces drew us together. The first was our mutual interest in Theosophy and two major religions, Buddhism and Hinduism. The second was music. Had I then known of Toby's interest in ballet and poetry, our links might have been closer. Both of us knew Arnold Haskell well. He was at Trinity Hall and he used to come frequently to my rooms in Trinity College to be consoled by Chopin and energized by Beethoven. One day he came in full of excitement and

*Editor's note: Christmas Humphreys died in 1983.

peremptorily gave me twenty four hours notice to prepare a short programme for Alicia.

'Alicia?' I queried.

'Mehta,' said Haskell, 'Alicia is a genius! Pavlova's successor! You must mug up these four piano pieces for her dance recital I have arranged for tomorrow evening.'

How could I disappoint such a gentle, friendly soul? I mugged the four pieces, my back to the 'child dancing like a fairy', as I was afterwards told. The future Markova, as gracious as an angel, thanked me for what in my judgment was poor pianistry and presented me with a signed photograph. Arnold Haskell, as imperious on that occasion as dear Toby can be on his occasions, was most grateful and was instrumental in introducing me—a very fateful introduction—to Solomon, the pianist, in 1924, just as Toby, in 1958, out of great and timely kindness introduced me to a man whose practical help provided the opportunity to begin writing *The Heart of Religion*. What an unfoldment of karmic patterns!

My mother introduced Theosophy and vegetarianism to me in September 1914, during my schooldays in Colombo. We went every Sunday afternoon to the meetings at Hope Lodge, the only one in Ceylon, of the Theosophical Society, with headquarters at Adyar and Annie Besant as President. By saving, for several years, the 'tiffin money' intended for my lunch snack at school, it became possible to buy Madame Blavatsky's works—*Isis Unveiled, The Secret Doctrine, The Key to Theosophy, A Modern Panarion*, and some volumes of *Lucifer*—and works by Annie Besant, Leadbeater, and translations of *The Upanishads*, the *Bhagavad Gītā*, and Greek and European philosophy. *The Voice of the Silence* and Mabel Collins' *Light on the Path* were two gems. They all enthralled me. The magnificence of the cosmogenesis in *The Secret Doctrine*, as also in the Hindu *Purānas*, the Grand Plan of the Universe and the origin, evolution and destiny of man, were all very thrilling. The grandiose, the spiritual super-romance, seems to be as attractive to the Indian temperament as they have been to Toby with his definitely English temperament. But whilst the impelling force towards religion and philosophy in my case was a wholly happy one, in Toby's case it was the shattering traumatic experience of his brother's death in war in 1917. Buddhism and Theosophy helped to restore mental poise and heal his broken heart. Thus fate had forged the link of certain common beliefs before we met in Cambridge.

Reading science meant about five to seven hours work every day with lectures and labs. There was not much opportunity for personal meetings. But I distinctly remember one occasion when Toby amused all present. He described the sitting room of a mutual friend, a history student in St John's College: 'Everything exquisite—curtains, carpet, cushions, chairs; books, desk, decorative objects, pictures, all in apple-pie order; a piano, a gramophone, and *millions of records*! Toby's 'millions' were in fact just about two dozen. But his ringing baritone voice produced the inevitable karmic result—laughter!

We trod different ways after Cambridge. Mine was learning the piano under Solomon for eight and a half years, and theory and composition under John Foulds. The learning was sheer happiness, but I had to discover the hard way that music was not my true vocation. Toby followed in his famous father's footsteps, and touched the peaks. He married and realized the joy and beauty of wedded life, except for the absence of children. True and happy marriage is a powerful influence for human good, a magic potion for dissolving at least some of the *dukkha* of humanity. What Puck Humphreys meant to Toby is expressed with poignant beauty in his autobiography, *Both Sides of the Circle* (London 1981; p. 246), in the lines written after her death:

FOR PUCK

One half of what for long was we
Has lived and loved and died again,
Leaving until we meet again
Only the tedium of me.

How the starkness of that tedium strikes the reader! A starkness as unanswerable as the starkness of death itself. The death of his brother in 1917 catapulted him on a certain road of which he says in his fascinatingly written autobiography (p. 32): 'From that hour I began a journey, and it has not ended yet, a search for the purpose of the universe, assuming it has one, and the nature of the process by which it came into being.' The death of Puck was an important milestone on 'the journey which has not ended yet'. Death struck again with the car crash which killed a beloved friend from early days, Irene, Lady Burton.

•

'Purpose' exists only in the context of duality (or multiplicity), in which there can be relationships, which define 'purpose', between one and an other (or others). 'Universe' implies the absolute unity, the one alone—there is no otherness in it, no others because of whose existence there can be relationships, and hence, 'purpose'-ful interactions. Death taught me this lesson. Hence I see that the Universe (or the Primordial Creative Power, or the Unborn, Unoriginated, Unformed) has no purpose which I, a finite mortal can perceive or formulate. But death also taught me that if I live *here-now* in such manner that the Totality fulfils itself as man (and the ultimate meaning of *hu-man* is *blissful creator*) through my existential being, my mortal life-span has fulfilled the *raison d'être* of its being. And so there is 'purpose' because of relationship and interaction between the separate self (the existential me) and the immense 'not-self'.

•

Puck Humphreys was a remarkable lady, possessed of many gifts, chief among them being the adoration of her husband. Year after year at the Buddhist Summer Schools at High Leigh at Hoddesden in Hertfordshire, one of my most delightful experiences was to watch the change of expression on Puck's face as she heard the President-Founder proclaim the same grand truths for the umpteenth time but with that magic touch he has of making it sound always as if it were the first time. There was no mistaking the light of love as it streamed from her shining eyes to her husband. He was her hero, her man, her beloved teacher and leader whom she would follow to the end of her days! Fortunate Toby! And blessed Puck to have been wife to the man who enabled her to share and to contribute in rich measure to all the joint triumphs in so many spheres. They walked on the pathway of the stars, hand in hand, for forty-eight years.

Even as Toby is devoted and faithful where he loves, he is staunch and generous as a friend, especially to one in genuine need. He may roar like a lion or growl like a bear at times, or pass severe sentence upon a law-breaker. But there is a compassionate heart withal—as when he tries to help the wrong-doer in prison to see that his own wrong-doing—and not the judge on the bench—brought him to this sorry pass.

It was Toby's destiny to enable the tender sapling of Buddhism in the Western world to grow firm and powerful roots and spread vigorous branches: a destiny which has been fulfilled. Toby is a true and outstandingly Buddhistic missionary, free of the slightest trace of militancy. He has his preference for Zen, since it suits his temperament; but the platform he offers at the Buddhist Society and its Summer Schools is a completely open platform for all forms of Buddhism and in fact for all truly religious religions—that is, for those whose source is Transcendence and whose teachings, if practised, liberate man from all bondage, ignorance and evil. Several years ago I was invited to give a series of talks on the disciplines of four major religions—Zarathushtrianism, Hinduism, Buddhism and Christianity. This was only one indication of the openness of this platform.

•

In the 3rd century BC, the Indian Emperor Aśoka (who had turned Buddhist in about 266 BC)—perhaps the most remarkable philosopher-king in all history—was so moved by the horrors and miseries of a war he waged in 262 BC to suppress the rebellious Kalingas on the east coast (modern Bihar), that he actively practised his Buddhism, ruled all India in accordance with Buddhist principles, especially compassion, and sent four missions westwards to lands which had Greek rulers as the result of Alexander's conquests, expressly to exhort their peoples to live their own faith more religiously and not to convert them to Buddhism. Although the missions gave rise to some good results, Buddhism did not take deep roots in these lands. Aśoka referred to himself in his Rock Edicts as *devanampiye* (favoured of the gods) *priyadarśin* (one who regards all with kindness), and as *rājā* (king), not as *mahārājā* (emperor).

Aśoka sent his own son and daughter, Mahinda and Sanghamitta, southwards to Sri Lanka. Here the result was different and endures to this day. Theravāda Buddhism flourished richly, spreading across south-east Asia. Whilst the admirable and indispensable work of British and European scholars first introduced the Buddha and his teachings to small interested groups in the 19th century in the West, and the devoted efforts of men like Dharmapala, Ananda Metteyya (the English monk Allan Bennett) and a few others in the early part of our century fostered this interest, brilliantly supported by the fine scholarship of the Rhys Davids, F. L. Woodward, E. M. Hare, Edward Conze and I. B. Horner, it is the life work of *karma-yogin* Toby Humphreys, the English *devanampiye*, which has definitely and securely placed Buddhism on the map of the Western world, even as Mahinda and Sanghamitta did for the Asian world twenty-two centuries ago. In Toby's personality were combined the requisite qualities and skills and energies which could lead to such a consummation.

So let us greet Toby, the Good Friend (see the *Sigālovāda Sutta*, No. 31 of the *Dīgha Nikāya*), with a cheerful and loving *Namaste!* on this his eightieth birthday, and wish him good health, happiness and deep serenity for all the years to come before he gracefully bids us the farewell from which there is no return. Thereafter, the name TOBY will be clearly visible to all who can read the *ākāśic* records.

Jāratkārava Ārtabhaga asked: Yājñavalkya, when such a man (*puruṣa* or *uttara puriso*) dies, what does not leave him?
Yājnavalkya answered: The name. Endless verily is the name. Endless are the All-gods (*viśve devas*). An endless world he wins thereby.

(*Bṛhadāraṇyaka Upanishad*, 3.2.12)

The Meaning of Death

(1982)

THE ORIGIN, a unitary whole, is primordial undifferentiated creative energy (not to be understood as any of the forms of energy known to science). It is infinite, self-replenishing, inexhaustible, indestructible. The Origin is also pure awareness, and fundamental substance (quite immaterial). These three named potencies—energy, awareness, substance—designate the one single Origin, just as John Michael Smith (and each name has its distinctive meaning) identifies one single person.

The unitary whole rests in vibrant quiescence—vibrant because alive; quiescent because all its potencies are in equilibrium, in unconstrained freedom and perfect order. This equilibrium is rocked by a stir of Transcendence in eternity—the primal act—karma. Thereupon, undifferentiated creative energy differentiates and simultaneously pure awareness proliferates complementarily and interactively. Grades of awareness-being emerge, interfused in each other and fully inter-related to one another, preserving the unity of the One Total Reality. These grades, beyond all ordinary sense-perception, have distinctive powers that function universally.

One of these grades is mind, that cosmic archetypal expression of energy-awareness which plays the directive rôle when the cosmos, of which our observable universe is only a fragment, comes into being.

The primal transcendental karma has no cause-effect sequence in it, no beginning-proceeding-ending, no birth-death. It is free, blissful creativity in eternity. It has no form, no measurability, no limitations. It is a discontinuous creative pulse, non-repetitive in so far as it does not give rise to the same creation as any other pulse. There is constant, incredibly swift renewal, trans*mutatively* not trans*formatively*. There is a new totality with every pulse (karma's transcendental functioning), which is the meaning of 'the complete working out' of karma. Where eternity is concerned, there is neither time nor succession; only immediacy. So too in our worldly, mortal sphere, but in terms of time and succession. Because it happens with extreme rapidity, our sluggish consciousness is unable to be aware of the complete working out of karma from moment to moment.

We may call this pulse of creation the life-death pulse in which life and death are simultaneous. But here death is the transmuter, not the ender. Preferably then we should call the pulse of creation the life/new-life pulse.

By this action in eternity, the immaterial fundamental substance, compressed into a single pin-point, bursts open explosively and becomes our universe of space-time-mass-energy (the forms of energy known to science), displaying infinite variety—the one as the many, the countless many as the indivisible one. This universe, the apparatus through which the Origin manifests itself, is wholly perishable. Marvellous though it may be, it is merely 'one garment of the Lord'. We humans, as multitudes of existential beings (*rūpa* to *viññāṇa*), are similarly the wholly perishable: the numerous 'garments' of the one imperishable *attā* or *ātman* (the transcendent *non-being*)—do not say 'Self'; in English, 'self', quite sensibly, means just the perishable psycho-physical organism. All beings, identifiable entities, are absorbed at death into the one all-pervasive non-being and are completely divested of separate identity—like rivers or raindrops merging into the ocean. The one non-being emanates, or presses out of itself, numerous existential beings, all of whom are *new* beings.

Consider the procreative process. Each parent produces a gamete (a mature reproductive cell). The process of development of a gamete, male or female, differs from that of a non-reproductive cell, for it involves *the rearrangement of the genetic material* inherited by each parent from their parents. The union of the male and female gametes produces a zygote, which becomes the new individual, different from the parents and from any person that ever was, is, or will be. He is a *new* creation, with *new* possibilities of mental development dependent on his environment and physical development. This is not a transference or carrying over of karma or character from a pre-existent person and is incompatible with any theory of re-incarnation.

Furthermore, our psychical life of thought and feeling depends upon the interaction of the parts of the highly complex nervous system and the influence of the endocrines. At death, the brain and central nervous system, and with them the whole life-record of thought and feeling, are obliterated. We die completely—the one act no one can avoid performing completely! The Buddha did teach that all five *skandhās, rūpa* to *viññāṇa*, are *anicca*. They all perish. Perhaps this is why in the *brahmavihāra* meditation we are told not to direct *mettā* or *karunā* to a dead person; it is the existential being who is in suffering and needs compassion, not the Origin which subsumes him and is embodied in him.

When fundamental substance bursts open, the influence of the formative, order-producing power of mind releases a cosmos with a streak of chaos running through it. Chaos supplies the challenge and impetus for striving, inquiry, experimentation, understanding and coming to fruition through progressive change by obedience to law. Only a part of this cosmos (the macroscopic) operates in terms of cause and effect, not the sub-atomic realm, in relation to which the traditional concepts of cause and effect, and of space and time, are meaningless in modern particle physics. The cosmos is constrained by Law that guides and ultimately presents it, liberated, back to Origin. We do not know the karmic law in its fullness. That aspect of it which we call cause and effect is the lord of process on the large scale, and even that is dimly understood and inadequately expounded.

The emergence and functioning of cosmos introduces the context of existence with which we are familiar, namely, the finite, temporal and mortal. This is fully subsumed in the context of Transcendence; namely, the infinite, eternal and immortal—the not-born, not-become, not-made, not-compounded, as affirmed by the Buddha. By the primal act—the stir of Transcendence in eternity—the Origin, by constricting Itself, ejects an involutionary swirl and the grades of awareness-being emerge. When, at the same instant, fundamental substance bursts open and cosmos is released, then beginning-proceeding-ending; birth-death; conflict, confusion and ignorance; all duality and multiplicity and evil make their appearance.

As involution proceeds, energy continues to concretize and awareness to be imprisoned in greater and greater degree, till the most dense and unenlightened state is reached in the mineral kingdom—complete earthiness. But consider the diamond, flashing with the promise of perfection of the Origin, for even the concretest, least awakened state in the cosmos is the embodied Origin, brought into being by its own primal act (karma). Earth, however, is the mother of life and the evolutionary process: through plant and animal there is lessening density of structure, growing refinement and sensitivity, exquisite complexity rooted in and based upon simple principles, and deeper awakening of consciousness.

There is an important implication here. The context of the infinite/eternal/immortal is wholly interfused with the context of the finite/temporal/mortal. What is even more important is that each and every finite particular in the entire cosmos, from an atom to a galaxy, a virus to a perfected holy one, is permeated through and through by the *whole* of infinity, by *all* of eternity. We cannot slice up infinity or eternity and appropriate bits for our finite selves any more than we can carve out slabs of space and screw our nameplates on them.

So we can see that statements like 'my' immortal spirit, or *ātman*, or soul are incorrect statements. Nevertheless, the immortal proves its immortality through the mortal who has utterly purified himself; i.e. deathlessness manifests unobstructedly through the death of all grasping and of every vestige of the consciousness and activity of separate selfhood.

Here, death is the purifier and liberator by being the destroyer of unskill and evil.

Science, having extensively investigated matter and the forms of energy we know, has shown that matter is electrical in origin and that mass and energy are interconvertible. So the age-old separating wall between the 'immaterial' and the 'material' has become so brick-bare that we can perceive unitary wholeness freely without encountering this wall. The world-view of modern scientists inclines increasingly towards a unitary wholeness; e.g. 'Undivided Wholeness in Flowing Movement' (*Wholeness and the Implicate Order*, p. 11, by Prof. David Bohm London: RKP, 1980).

The erstwhile 'immutable Laws of Nature' which hold on the macroscopic scale are not obeyed in the sub-atomic realm. Uncertainty and probability prevail here and have shaken the 'fixed order of things'. Strict causality is one of the major casualties. We *must* revise our understanding of the law of karma.

Change—the constant universal phenomenon—may be (1) *Fortuitous*, and apparently of no significance or value; (2) *Regressive*: deterioration, decrepitude, decay; (3) *Progressive*: improvement, growth, fruition, culmination; (4) *Final*; death as a gentle ender or violent destroyer, or, death which is perfecter, consummator, transmuter.

The karmic process is the living process of the ceaselessly changing universe as a whole. Whilst confined to *viññāṇa* (discriminative, analytical consciousness) which prevents the functioning while we are alive of 'pure all-inclusive awareness shining everywhere' (the *viññāṇaṃ anidassanaṃ anantaṃ sabbatopabhaṃ* of *M*.1.329, the Buddha's equivalent of the *ātman*; see especially the *Varāha Upanishad*, 2.21), we think fragmentarily and speak incorrectly when we say 'my' karma or 'your' karma. *It is karma in its totality which has you or me, not you or I who have karma*. The prevailing state of the universe at any instant changes into the next state by the very next split second. Death and rebirth play their parts. In our personal life as existential beings, how does rebirth take place? Because of the ceaselessness of change, the prevailing state dies. Here, death is the ender. Karma, now functioning as cause-effect sequence and not transcendentally because it is operating in the existential sphere of the finite and temporal, releases the changed state. Excepting the perfected holy ones, all of us are isolatively and separatively self-conscious (*self* meaning the five-aggregate bundle) in terms of 'I am I and not any other person or thing'. The ordinary I-am-I consciousness is indispensable for our everyday life. It is this 'and not any other person or thing' which is the root of evil and endless conflict, for it denies the fact of our complete inter-relationship with the universe.

Furthermore, if we scrutinize intently and clear-sightedly (assuming of course that we have the faultless ability to do so) what exactly we are referring to when we say 'I am I', we shall see that this 'I' is no other than one or more or even all of the five *skandhās*, for the *skandhās* are all that we are really conscious of. Words like 'God', '*ātman*', 'Creative Spirit', 'divine spark', etc., are but symbols, arbitrary assertions, not conscious realizations. We may sincerely asseverate that this 'I' refers to the *attā*. But persevere with the scrutiny and we will discover it is not the *attā* to which we are actually referring, for if it were, our 'I-am-I' consciousness would be the totality-embracing, transcendent pure awareness, and therefore our daily thinking-feeling-speaking-doing would naturally and spontaneously manifest Transcendence. Does it?

Therefore, our isolative self-consciousness, which arises quite some time after our birth as the result of our circumstantial conditioning and which functions right through our waking and dream states, but which remains quiescent whenever the organism is in sound dreamless slumber or in a deep *jhāna*, which re-associates itself with the organism when the body wakes up again and which survives *only as long as* all five *skandhā* hold together as the living existential being—this 'I-am-I' is indeed only existential and completely perishes with the perishing of the organism.

In our daily life we continuously associate this 'I' with every thought, feeling, mood, action, etc. So we helplessly say, out of our ignorance, '*I* think, feel, do, etc.* *When*

*The word 'I' is a linguistic convenience in practical daily life. As such, all the holy ones used it freely. The frequency and tone-quality of the word as used by most of us is a reliable measure of our egoism.

the prevailing state or action has come to its end, 'I' have died. Immediately afterwards the 'I-am-I' self-consciousness associates itself with, and is lord of the next state. So, 'I' am reborn and die and am reborn countless times during the single lifetime of the organism. How profoundly significant is the Buddha's affirmation on the twenty-first night after the Enlightenment: 'He who doth crush the great "I am" conceit,* this, truly this, is happiness supreme' (*Mahāvagga*, 3.4).

Now, if in our own lives the emergence of the new state is to be a perfect, healthy birth, we have to die healthily; i.e. die wholly and voluntarily to the prevailing state. No grasping at the new: no clinging to the perishing old. Thus we cease to be *miserable* perishers! Thus, too, proper growth takes place. We see, then, why the Buddha emphasized that we should not cling to *rūpa* or *vedanā* or *saññā* or *saṃkhārā* or *viññāṇa*. The entire existential being dies from moment to moment during its lifetime, and completely so with the final end of the psycho-physical organism.

Here, death is the destroyer, gentle or violent, according to the circumstance.

Hence of no *skandhās* can it be said: 'This is mine, this am I, this is the *attā* of (or within) me.' The Buddha taught that each and every one of the five *skandhā* composing the whole of the existential being should be seen with wise, perfect insight as 'This is not mine, this am I not, this is not the *attā* of me.'

There are two implications here: (1) 'I' (*ahaṃ*) as used by all the perfected holy ones, is identical with the *attā*, and (2) the *attā* is the imperishable, birthless and deathless. Its context is the infinite, eternal, immortal. (The commentary on the *Udāna*, p. 340, explains *tathāgata* by *attā*.)

Thus death operates continuously throughout our existential life. So does rebirth in—and only in—the sense and context explained above. In the *Visuddhimagga* (p. 625, Bhikkhu Ñānamoli's translation: Kandy, Sri Lanka, 1979), Buddhaghosa writes: 'When a man is confused about death, instead of taking death thus, "Death in every case is the break-up of aggregates" (*rūpa* to *viññāṇa*), he figures

*Here, 'conceit' means a fanciful, unreal notion.

that it is a lasting being that dies, that it is a lasting being's transmigration to another incarnation and so on. When he is confused about reappearance, instead of taking rebirth thus, "Birth in every case is the manifestation of aggregates", he figures that it is a lasting being's manifestation in a new body. When he is confused about the round of rebirths, instead of taking the round of rebirths thus, "The endless chain of aggregates, of elements, of bases too, that carries on unbrokenly is called the round of births", he figures that it is a lasting being that goes from this world to another world, that comes from another world to this world.'

All the above may cause distress, produce painful perplexity. Questions will arise: If there is no reincarnation, how can my karma be worked out in a single lifetime? How can I possibly perfect the *sīlas* and *pāramitās*, become proficient in *samādhi*, grow in faultless insight (*paññā*), destroy the cankers (*āsavā*), become a *bodhisattva*, attain Buddhahood, realize Nirvana?

Are not all these questions self-orientated— therefore defeating any chance of seeing the truth? Do they not betray 'my' egoism and vanity, lust and greed, illusions and delusions, fears and stupidity? If and when you loved truly, purely, transcendentally (which is the ultimate meaning of *humanly*) did you ask, expect, hope for anything from the beloved for yourself? Or did you give your whole self, unreservedly and unconditionally to the beloved?

Do not worry about your karma. The universe will see to it! As already said, it works itself out completely from split second to split second. We all know that our moods, feelings, thoughts, etc., are intimately linked with the electro-chemistry of the body, promoting health or producing disease according to whether our psychical activity is skilled or unskilled. Again, throughout the day we experience the effects of our choices, decisions, judgements, attentiveness, mindfulness, etc., etc. Furthermore, we must remember that not one of us is solely and exclusively responsible for the thoughts and feelings, words and actions in our daily life. The whole world is involved in whatsoever proceeds out of us or befalls us. Being blind to the *dukkha* wrought by the isolativeness and separativeness of our self-consciousness, we resent this and think it is unjust. But the factual living process of the universe— karma—takes no notice of our concepts of justice. We are imperfect humans, prisoners of *avidyā* and *taṇhā*, *sub*-humans still growing towards true humanness.

If you are still worried, consider these points. Transcendence embodied in you has no existential karma. When the five-*skandhā* bundle dies, all the physical atoms composing the body return to the universal stock, all the psychical components likewise return to the aggregates, affecting and influencing the quality and properties of the stock. Each of us is thus responsible for all, and all for each.

Not a single one of these countless atoms or psychical components is labelled *John* or *Mary*. If you have been an evil person, posterity may recall your name with sorrow; if good, with love; if a perfected holy one, with adoration. When a new individual is born, the stuff composing him is drawn out of the worsened or improved universal store of atoms and psychical components. All the Johns and Marys and creatures and plants and the very earth itself of the whole past of the world are contributors to the new babe. The new babe is the rebirth of the totality, not of 'you' or 'me'. The One is in the multitude; the multitude is in each and every one, and in The One. Truth is *a*-rational, fully subsuming rationality and irrationality.

We may take a deeper view. Infinity and eternity wholly subsume the existential. Within eternal Transcendence, the existential lives and moves and has its temporal being. Transcendence never compels—it has no need to do so. Compulsion is manifest only in the sphere of the perishing relative. But Transcendence and the relative affect each other. We as mortals leave an impress by our whole life-activity upon Transcendence. The relative has no creative power except biologically, and that too only pro-creatively. Transcendence *is* creative energy. Our imperfections (failures) necessitate new expressions in the finite and mortal sphere of the relative by the creative power of Transcendence. Thus *karma works holistically*; but the new expressions are not *re*-incarnations. The originality of the divine craftsman is inexhaustible. An ancient teaching affirms that the universe is the son of necessity. Meditate on it.

Karma is not concerned with 'rewarding' the good and 'punishing' the bad (ponder deeply on the first two verses of the *Dhammapada*), nor with 'balancing the accounts' for each separate person. Karma works holistically *for the fruition of the Whole*. Transcendence is the immortal doer and final reaper, not mortal 'you' or 'I', the finite, temporal garments of the Origin. The true function of karma is to *heal*, literally to *make holy* that fragment of totality which is bruised, ill and crazy, and enable it to be re-integrated into the Origin. Thus indeed divine justice is done.

In his *Nicomachean Ethics* (Book 5, Chapter 2), Aristotle said, 'Justice is *the practice of perfect Virtue towards others as well as oneself*'. How perfectly this is in harmony with the Buddha's teachings (see, for example, *The Parable of the Saw*, M.1.128, 129) and with the *Sermon on the Mount* by Jesus (Matthew, chapter 5)!

Consider with a heart at peace (i.e. un-self-concerned) this story:

> The Divine Justiciar, Almighty Lord of Karma, said to his devotee crouching by Thames bank:
>
> 'My child, what are you doing there?'
>
> 'Counting the drops of water, father.'
>
> 'Why?'
>
> 'To balance the accounts due from the water-pot bearers.'
>
> 'Come away, dear child, and desist from fruitless toil. I pour out the Holy Water of Eternal Life, and all are made Whole by that tide. I open the heart of Compassion and Wisdom, and all enter into everlasting bliss. In my House of Songs, none sweats at accounts—my twin brother, Death, sees to all that. Beloved Child! come thou in and sing me a sweet song. And Nirvana's Peace will enfold you.'

If you truly long to awaken to truth and not stop short at 'signed-on-the-dotted-line' membership of the Buddhist (or any other religious) fold, live the holy life, the *Brahmacarīya*. Its heart is *sammā sati*, perfect mindfulness every moment of your life, waking and sleeping. When *sati* climaxes in supreme intensity, you will be in rhythm with the karmic process from moment to moment, and you will experience death as new-life. This is the realization of deathlessness by Transcendence in and through you, the unobstructing perfected holy one. Here death the new-life, 'become one with the Supreme' (in the words of the *Subāla Upanishad,* 11, 13, 15) is the perfecter and consummator.

'You' or 'I', finite and mortal, can never enter Nirvana, for we would only 'stain the white radiance of eternity' by our passion to remain identifiable entities. In Nirvana, in the context of infinity and eternity, there are no separate identifiable entities. But when we take the Lord of Death right into our hearts, new-life completely dissolves finitude and mortality. All isolative self-consciousness disappears, transmuted into the all-inclusive pure awareness of the Origin. Death, the Lord of the Hidden Light, gives us the kiss of life immortal. Thereupon, only the Origin, Transcendence alone *is*. Thus death is the divine transmuter, Śiva the Auspicious.

These are all words. But meditate on them till they wither away by springing to life as fully awakened pure awareness. Then you will realize death as the sweet honey spread on your slice of the bread of life.

The Nature of Meditation

(1983)

THROUGHOUT the ages there have always been people who were profoundly concerned with the deep questions of life. What or who is the ultimate real? They were concerned with questions about the source, the end, the meaning and the purpose of their lives. They were deeply disturbed by what they could see of life as it was: its extraordinary mystery, sorrow, pain, and conflict, on one hand; its pleasure, joy and ecstasy, on the other. They wondered what was the answer to all these questions. Was there the possibility for men to realize peace and freedom, liberation from the ambivalent and embattled condition in which we all live? They found their answers and that finding was in their continuous living of the particular answer they had found. This is a very important point, for we are apt to think of the answer as a message, an idea, a doctrine, a system of philosophy, a way of life, a practice and a method, instead of a continuous awakening: a living here and now.

They arrived at their answers in a very interesting way. They discovered that when body and mind were both pacified—not suppressed but at peace, at ease—they experienced a state of communion in which isolative self-consciousness was absent. In the absence of isolative self-consciousness the state of communion was a realization, a making real, of Transcendence: not only in terms of an 'I' which was related to a 'you' or an 'it' but a state of wholeness in which the differentiation between the 'I' and the 'you' or 'it' as subject-and-object was completely overleaped.

It is important for us to grasp this clearly because such communion is the supreme meditative state, the real meaning of being in *samādhi*. It is the end of the turmoil of the imperfect mind, of all self-orientated discursive thought, of all image-making, of all striving. It is peace, the fullness of Being realized in every single moment of life in which there is no 'I' that becomes this, that or the other. In that supreme communion there is no 'I'. Hence this state cannot be sought or found. It supervenes when there is no obstruction in you to oppose it. It is not something that you can attain or achieve. It *is* the infinite. How can anyone attain or achieve the infinite? It is everlastingly here, now. It is the ungraspable immeasurable. Can you take your foot-rule and measure the universe? Transcendence, the infinite, is the One Total Reality. If and when I am clean, still and silent, empty of illusions and confusion, then that unknown Transcendence functions freely and fully in me. It manifests itself as fulfilled hu-manhood, as the perfected holy life of the individual who is free from all isolative self-consciousness. In him is seen the complete reversal of all worldliness. The perfected one lives in the world but has ceased to be of the world, not by retreating from the world but by being free of all the opposites which constitute our ambivalent life: attachment-aversion, attraction-repulsion, taking sides with what we imagine to be the good against what we call the evil, and so forth.

Now meditation is the natural and supreme discipline of the religious mind. Discipline means learning through observing with an open mind. Our conditioned minds are not open. If you watch your mental processes very carefully, you will see that every single stimulus which reaches you is interpreted by you in accordance with your particular conditioning: your own judgements, evaluations, criteria and values; your beliefs, convictions and experience. All of them have some validity in the dualistic sphere of opposites in conflict with each other. They have no validity whatsoever in terms of Transcendence. In the context of the infinite, all our values and criteria disappear.

In actual fact we are always in the infinite but are unaware of it. The marvel of the unitary infinite is its manifestation in terms of multitudinousness; an extraordinary, unimaginable, incalculable variety of unique particulars which are all in relationship with each other all the time, partly knowingly but largely unknowingly; and it is this which makes up that totality which is the whole, the infinite; which never decreases, never increases; which is dimensionless, immeasurable. But we observe with minds that are cramped; we don't observe wholly and completely in the immediate present. We always compare our observation with something else we know, with something of the past. All our perceptions are cramped, imprisoned by our fixed concepts. We do not perceive as if it were for the first time each and every time we look. Therefore our relationship with that which is perceived is an incomplete relationship. And because of comparison and judgement and criticism, attachment and aversion, the choosing of pleasure against pain and so forth, we remain in a state of conflict, of disharmony. Discipline means observing with a completely open mind all the time. Then you discover for yourself in every observation that you make, and in that type of discovery you really understand. Real understanding is not a matter of having certain ideas about what you experience. Ideas are merely strings of words. Understanding is a positive, active communion with that which you are observing and therefore this understanding born of uncovering Truth is real wisdom and, simultaneously, true love. The relationship, the unity between the observed and the observer, is complete. So you see that discipline is not sticking to a laid-down method which is mechanically observed and followed, something of the nature of a regular routine in order to produce a desired, preconceived end. It is precisely because we bend our energies to obtaining a desired, preconceived end that we meet with frustration, with sorrow, and are in the ill state

Why does one turn to religion? Generally because one is in sorrow, in difficulty; one has been frustrated, hurt; one has tried this and tried that. Finally one turns to religion in order to find comfort and satisfaction. He himself, whose mind is hurt, tortured, broken; whose mind is confused, ignorant; whose intellect is the slave of desire—how can such a person form or have a preview of that which is the truly happy, the truly peaceful state? It is impossible. But this is precisely what everyone does. If anyone, consciously or unconsciously but exploitatively, says to you: 'Follow this method and you will find the desired goal; you will find heart's desire fulfilled, Nirvana, the Kingdom of Heaven' and so forth—be very careful. Avoid him. But if you do discover for yourself and understand, then your natural wisdom is released from the burden of acquired knowledge, doctrines, systems of philosophy and teachings. The collections of ideas with which we stuff our minds are a burden of acquired knowledge. All one will have to do ultimately is cast them aside. The Buddha himself taught unequivocally that the wise man sees clearly for himself that all feelings, all material shapes and forms, all ideas, all patterns of thought and even discriminative consciousness itself are impermanent, the very source of suffering, not ultimate reality.

The religious mind is concerned with Transcendence, which is not a thing, an object, something which one separates from the totality. As I said earlier, I am using the word 'Transcendence' in the meaning of the *One Total Reality*, whatsoever it may be. What produces all the trouble is my own state of confusion. That is why I am not conscious of totality as if it were second nature to me. I am not conscious of it in its wholeness. Not being conscious of it in its wholeness—and also for other causes such as taking sides with one thing against another—I remain in a state of conflict with no way out. The religious mind, then, concerned with Transcendence, is concerned with truth as a whole and constant living experience here and now. Not an isolated experience which you will talk about and flaunt for the rest of your lifetime—'That was my enlightenment'. Such a phrase would be untrue; the very word 'my' betrays its untruth. You or I as mortal finite entities can never be fully enlightened. Only when the finite *you* has dissolved as the result of the complete transmutation of isolative self-consciousness and there is only awareness of totality as totality—only then is the perfectly enlightened state present, manifested through you. The infinite immortal Reality is manifest through you, the finite mortal reality.

Certain clarifications are necessary at this point; otherwise whatever we consider will inevitably be misconsidered. It is a great mistake to approach meditation in order to solve personal problems. The world process continually throws up challenges, whatever you are, whoever you are. Our individual task is to meet such challenges in the right way: selflessly, intelligently; free from the drive of particular desires and objectives. How do we usually meet the challenges of the world? 'This is painful to me; it is difficult for me—I want to be rid of it.' The whole world says that and thus lives daily in the fear of suffering. Life has to be a continuous learning, not a getting rid of the undesirable and the unpleasant which will inevitably come to each and every one of us. If we have good sense, we will not try to get rid of trouble but learn from it and understand it while it lasts. Any condition, however troublesome, however painful, inevitably ends. But if I struggle against it and end it prematurely—or, worse still, succeed in bringing about what I think to be a pleasant situation—then I will not have learned from it. I will die an ignorant man in the end.

The great question is: *How shall I live through my years, dying continuously in the right way*? Because that is what determines my next state of awareness here and now during my lifetime. All my cycles of birth and death take place in my lifetime, from moment to moment. It is the transformation of this moment-to-moment awareness of existence which spells the enlightened state, otherwise the ordinary state of *dukkha* continues. So, how shall I die? Shall I burn away like a fire that is belching forth smoke all the time? Or shall I burn like a pure flame, a pure light which sheds a friendly warmth around? How can I do that unless I refuse to get rid of troublesome things, unless I become free from chasing after what seem to me to be pleasant things? The Buddha taught *upekkhā*, the ordinary meaning of which is *indifference*; but he taught *upekkhā* as the culmination of love. How do you square indifference with transcendental love? If I myself, or you yourself, are free from attachment to the pleasant and of aversion to the unpleasant; if you have ceased to take sides with one thing against another—then, with a free mind, you can clearly see all the aspects concerned. Then only, indifferent to all duals, understanding begins. Otherwise there is no understanding, and in that absence there can be no love. There can be attachment, passion, fancy, conceit, illusion, but not love.

So one has to avoid the mistake of approaching meditation in order to solve personal problems. They usually dissolve in time. Who is the personalizer of any challenge which life throws down at me anyway? I myself, because I do not look at it as a whole being looking at a whole situation. My looking is blinkered by my own personal desires and preferences, and by the exercise of choice conditioned by my limitations and defilements. But if I am free from personal preferences and conditioned choice I can begin to see that 'my' problem is a universal problem—*dukkha* is universal and not a special visitation afflicting me alone, perhaps a few others as well. Then it becomes possible to see *dukkha* dispassionately, to truly understand it, to see it impersonally as if all humanity were seeing it—and thus see it with a heart matured by compassion. Therefore, on ceasing to be exclusively personal, the problem vanishes. One's own clear consciousness of truth affects all mankind for the good. Thus, free of any 'personal' problem, I can be in a state of true communion with the actual situation. That is meditation; that is the meditative condition.

Then again there are those who approach meditation in order to gain health, to acquire mental powers or to experience the super-sensible. People 'practise meditation', mistaking fantastic musing or verbal ritual for true meditation, in order that they may have wonderful higher-plane experiences. In reality they are probably incompetent at dealing with lower-plane or ordinary experiences! How they will deal with higher-plane experiences is a bit of a mystery! This passion to enjoy the super-sensible; to acquire this or gain that; to enjoy bliss, attain Nirvana or realize Transcendence—all these passions merely blind one and if one experiences something which seems to be good, which seems to indicate that, *'Ah, this means progress!'*, all that is happening is that one's ego is becoming more bloated.

You see, the real good, truth, love and wisdom are the innermost essences of your psycho-physical being. So now we must avoid the mistake of adopting any of these worldly approaches because they are all self-orientated: '*I' am going to gain, to achieve, to attain* . . . And the fact that they are self-orientated ensures their defeat.

The very concept that *I* or *he* will attain Nirvana is a false concept. The finite can never 'attain' the infinite. The inner reality is more like this: that the infinite comes to fruition through you. If you are clean, pure, silent, alert, awake, unresisting and infinitely resilient, then, when totality shines forth through you, absolutely unhindered, the organism will not break under the strain—just like an electric bulb which can take the voltage.

We must very clearly appreciate all this before we begin to attempt meditation in any serious, real sense. The truly religious mind approaches meditation in the spirit of the creative artist. Your artist can't help himself. The infinite made him that way, and because he gives himself completely to it, immortal beauty is therefore created by him. He is not an egoistic, self-conscious creator of beauty: '*I am making beauty*.' It is beauty which has come to manifestation through him and that is how it is with the person who wants to meditate. He cannot help himself but meditate and then, because he gives himself unconditionally, come what may Transcendence itself functions through him. And that is the meaning of Nirvana being present here-now. Not that somebody takes this step and that step and another step and finally reaches a gate labelled, *Nirvana: Enter Here*.

Now, the total giving of oneself to the religious life means essentially purification and meditation. Purification is closely knit to mindfulness. Mindfulness is, in fact, a continuous meditation. Purity is *the* indispensable basis or else meditation brings you to an ill state because it releases power—and that power or energy intensifies everything in your psyche, good and bad alike. So that if I am in a state of conflict—in which I *must* be if I have not transcended all ambivalence—what is commonly called good as well as what is commonly called bad is intensified in me and the struggle is worse than ever.

Notice how in one's life, say, one goes to church.

Everything is lovely. The sermon is inspiring, the cerimonial most affecting; one feels uplifted, calmed, at peace and so forth. Then one walks out of the church and stands in the bus queue. Somebody pushes past you; jumps the queue. Now see what happens to your sublime state! You are in a far greater rage than if you had not gone to church and been uplifted! It sounds amusing but it is a serious fact. We have to beware of this. Every release of power out of the world of mind simply energizes both aspects of our being as long as we are living ambivalently: the good and the bad alike.

Don't play with meditation. It is like fire. There must be a basis of purity first and foremost. If there is not that basis, you will only sentence yourself to frustration. The great teachers knew this very well. Therefore the Buddha laid down *sīla*, morality, as the preliminary preparation. He called it right conduct of body, speech and mind. Just right conduct. Practise it assiduously every day. First harmlessness: to abstain from taking the life of any creature and from harming any living thing. Next to abstain from taking that which is not given. The third is very important: to abstain from all sense-indulgence, not only indiscriminate sexuality. Make no mistake about this. Abstain from all sense-*indulgence*; the right use of the senses is quite a different thing. Only a truly *sensible* person uses his senses rightly. He would be a very incautious person who would say, 'I am really sensible.' We are all a little bit senseless and so we indulge the senses and bolster up our indulgence, our lack of perception. We bolster up the fact that we are a little conscience-stricken that we are living like sub-humans by saying, 'Oh, but modern psychologists have shown this, that and the other . . .' Look very carefully at what modern psychologists have shown. They have shown you that which will keep you in the sphere of worldliness and they make you a little bit more efficient in self-assertion and the gaining of self-orientated worldly success. All right, if that is what you want, carry on. But if you are concerned with meditation, with Transcendence, with something which means the true fruition of man in you, then let this psychologist be the exemplar first before he tries to show you the way. The psychologist is concerned with recirculating the worldling in the sphere of worldly affairs. The spiritual teacher is concerned with liberating you from this conflicting, ambivalent sphere into that state of complete wholeness in which totality has come to fruition through you and you are a light unto the world.

Next we come to the tremendous teaching about mindfulness; *sammā sati*, 'perfect mindfulness', as the Buddha put it. Now, perfect mindfulness is concerned with the specific aspects of meditation, particularly as a ground-work preparation for specific meditation. Mindfulness itself is a 24-hour-a-day meditation. It means being alert, being watchful, being awake to all your living experience here-now, from moment to moment. But be alert and watchful, free of criteria, evaluation, judgement, condemnation or approval. As you go through your experience watchfully you will find reactions springing up in your brain all the time. Watch those reactions. Not a single one has any warrant in the context of truth. There all our values, judgements, condemnations, etc., are useless.

Be free of them. If one watches these reactions as they spring up and just remains mindful—that is, intensely attentive—you will find that they are merely *saṇkhārā*: thought-patterns, patterns which condition us. They will dissolve away under that intense attentiveness.

It is this process of dissolution which is the purification. You cannot become pure by predetermining what purity is. There is nothing which the discursive mind throws up which is anything but a hindrance to the perfect communion between the finite mortal and infinite transcendent. Mental turmoil goes on ceaselessly in the brain in both the waking and dream states due to our conditioning. It is tied up with desire and our intellect acting as the slave of desire. It is this turmoil which is the constant block. When one sees through it and its power is dissolved away by intense attentiveness, then a new state of awareness of existence arises in you. There is a transformation of your consciousness by which it becomes transcendent awareness in which only the whole is present for you. In that state, you, the finite individual, become capable of absorbing the infinitude of impressions and indeed everything that comes to you, without rejecting anything or being tied to anything by acceptance. This brings about the liberated condition.

With such mindfulness operating continuously, there is continuous purification. Then you can practise the specific meditation which is the contemplative discipline through which all obstructiveness within oneself to the emergence of Transcendence is removed and the free flow of Transcendence through you can take place. These are the *jhānas* and *samāpattis.* They have been miscalled 'trances'. You are not in a trance in the *jhānas;* you are completely awake. Now, do not think that this awakened state is one in which discriminative consciousness functions: a state in which you are aware that *I,* the subject, am seeing *that,* the object. Because you have gone beyond the subject-object duality, it is impossible to describe that ineffable state. The Buddhist sacred texts—like the Hindu, Christian and other sacred texts—have always talked about it as the unthinkable, the unimaginable, the unpictureable, and, above all, as the ungraspable.

Now you can see why at the beginning I stressed the right approach, the *unselfed* approach. There is nothing for me to grasp as 'mine'. Through meditation, through the religious life, through what we call improvement and advancement, there is nothing whatsoever for *me,* the ordinary mortal manifested for a while in time and space. Whatever is for me is something I am vainly trying to grasp for myself and this lies at the very root of all evil in our lives. Understand this and you will understand why the Buddha said: 'Ananda, the freedom of the mind from all grasping is indeed Nirvana.'

When meditation has become your natural and spontaneous living state and when you, the purified individual, live in continuous relationship with the totality, then Transcendence realizes itself through you and you yourself are the living embodiment of the supreme, the undefinable, the inconceivable and the absolute. This is Nirvanic bliss.

Krishnamurti:

The Man, the Teacher and the Teaching

(1987)

A Review of *Krishnamurti: a Biography*, by Pupul Jayakar (Harper & Row: San Francisco, 1986) 516 pp. $22.95 (c £16.50)

KRISHNAMURTI often referred to himself as 'K' in his talks and dialogues. For convenience, let us use K in this review and P for his excellent biographer, a philosopher in her own right and a prominent social worker in her young days. A few words about her would not be out of place. The only dark-complexioned child out of five in a family where all were fair, P was very sensitive and timid. Many lonely hours were spent in reading books, seldom understood, and in hearing legends and tales about India. Happier were the walks with her Irish governess, learning about plants and flowers and enjoying stories of Arthur and Guinevere and British history. P went to college in England, met the Indian gentleman whom she married after returning to India, and was blessed with one daughter. Later on, turning away from housewifery, she plunged into the social and intellectual life of Bombay. There followed the agony of two unfortunate pregnancies, the deaths of an unborn child and of a deformed child, and 'the racking pain of her beloved father's death' (p. 5). This schooling in pain was her preparation for meeting the man who saw light through his own and the world's sorrows and showed the cure for it.

Such was the lady who, at the age of 32, first met K in January 1948 and became closely associated with his work till his death. In the late 1950s, K himself suggested that she should write a book on his life. Begun in 1978, it is based on P's notes and taped dialogues, and the available material from the archives of the Theosophical Society.

Forty seven chapters divided into six parts cover K's life and teaching: (1) The Early Years, 1895–1946; (2) in India, 1947–1949; (3) The Unfolding of the Teaching, 1950–1959; (4) Rivers of Insight, 1960–1962; (5) Changing Horizons, 1962–1977; (6) Summation of the Teaching, 1978–1985; a short Epilogue speaks of his death. P has the gift to unify the life and the teachings. K's life *is* his teachings and his teachings are the quintessential distillate of his whole life, a life of selfless service dedicated to Truth, that pathless land where he roamed so playfully, unconditionally free, and which he bequeathed to us so graciously.

On 12 May 1895 at 12.30 a.m. to Sanjeevamma, wife of Jiddu Naraniah, a son. Devout Sanjeevamma was psychic; she had visions and could see people's auras. In India, birth, death and the menstrual cycle are regarded as focuses of ritual pollution. But this mother of Light challenged the gods and shattered superstition by preparing and using for this birth—the shrine room! The birth was an easy one. He, the compassionate one-to-be, could not hurt anyone, even unwittingly. Next day, astrologer Kumara Shrowthulu predicted confidently that the boy would become a great teacher. The name-giving ceremony took place on the sixth day. True to brahminical tradition, this eighth child was named Krishnamurti after that other eighth child, Shri Krishna, the Incarnate Lord. Three years later Sanjeevamma bore Nityananda.

The two brothers, devoted to each other, grew up as two bodies animated by a single heart of love, but quite different in abilities. Nitya shone academically. K had no interest in academic work or worldly affairs and failed every examination for which he sat. Both had intelligence in their own different ways and both, physically, were weak and sickly. K suffered much illness throughout his life and died of cancer of the pancreas, at 12.10 a.m. on 17 February 1986; Nitya died of a serious attack of influenza in 1925. K's attention was absorbed by clouds, trees, flowers, insects and by mechanical contrivances like clocks, and later on in life, by cars.

Sanjeevamma's death in 1905 left K bewildered and bereft; his father, a Theosophist, retired in 1908. Unable to maintain the large family on a meagre income of round about £8 per month, Naraniah succeeded after preliminary difficulty in persuading Mrs Annie Besant (AB) the President of the Theosophical Society (TS) to let him work as assistant secretary to the Esoteric Section of the Society, in exchange for free accommodation in Adyar for himself and the family.

The family settled there in late January 1910. Less than three weeks later, Charles Leadbeater (CWL), who had come to Theosophy five years before AB and apparently had clairvoyant gifts, came to Adyar. K also, even as a boy, had psychic gifts like his mother's. He could read people's thoughts, or the contents of a closed letter, and could see auras; he also saw the forms of his dead sister and mother; but he took no special account of all this.

K and his brothers would go down to the beach in the evenings to paddle and to watch some of the Europeans in Adyar swim. One evening, CWL and his assistants went for a swim. He was most favourably impressed by the aura of one of the lads paddling on the beach. Returning from the swim, he told Ernest Wood about this most wonderful aura, which had not a particle of selfishness in it. The boy was Krishna. CWL was convinced that this was the vehicle through which the *bodhisattva* Maitreya would give the new teaching to the world. K and Nitya both came under the tutelage of the heads and leading members of the TS.

•

Madame Helena Petrovna Blavatsky (HPB), daughter of the aristocratic Colonel Peter Hahn, claimed to have lived in Tibet for several years close to the Masters of Wisdom: an occult group of spiritual teachers from whom she gathered the knowledge of well-guarded doctrines of Tibetan sages. Under their guidance, in 1873 she sought out Colonel Henry Steele Olcott, a psychic researcher like herself who had psychic gifts. They founded the TS in 1885, to form a nucleus of universal brotherhood, to study the Ancient Wisdom and to explore the mysteries of nature and the latent powers of man. Before her death in 1891, HPB had written that the real purpose of the TS was to prepare for the advent of the World Teacher. Whispers about the coming Messiah had spread among occult communities by the end of the 19th century. AB, one of the most remarkable women in our era, became President of the TS after Olcott's death in 1907 (p. 23). After CWL's 'discovery' of K, she and CWL took charge of K's and Nitya's education and training. The object was to prepare the body of K to become a fit instrument through which the Bodhisattva Maitreya (the Lord) could once again teach mankind (cf. the *Bhagavad Gita*, 4.7,8). Theosophists expected that when the Lord spoke through K, He would support, clarify and advance the doctrines and practices promulgated by the TS.

It happened that K developed into an original seer and teacher. We must note that precisely this sets the stamp of teacherhood on K, for the teachings of all the true spiritual teachers are outstandingly distinguished by the *originality* of their presentation of the Truth. This has to be the case because of the unique conditions and culture of every new age. The teachers were always concerned with man's salvation and with the flowering of man's human-ness (which is the same as man's divinity and creativeness). The originality of the teaching spells the freedom of the teacher.

K went through a terrible preparatory ordeal (see pages 46–57) before standing on the peak of freedom. It has been called 'the Process', very painful physically, starting in August 1922 and continuing to November 1923, repeating on and off a few times till 1927. It is thought that 'the Process' was the raising of the serpent fire of *kundalinī* yoga and the opening of the third eye. In addition to 'the Process', he suffered a ghastly trauma whilst travelling by sea to India when he heard the news of the death of his brother Nitya in California. For ten days K was beside himself with grief: his grief, world grief. He came out of it a new man, the teacher, or, in his own words, 'He who held out the Light of Truth'.

Thus was K weaned away from beliefs, doctrines, dogmas and authority. He was very strongly against accepting anything on mere authority. His attitude was,

'I wonder if this is true. Let me investigate and find the truth for myself.' Investigate; know for myself, nothing on hearsay—we are reminded of the Buddha. K was freeing himself of his conditioning since his 'discovery' by CWL. He spoke of 'The Beloved', his teacher: Life itself. Nearly four more years were to elapse before this free man dissolved the burden of a vast organization of over 40,000 members all over the world—the Order of the Star—built by AB and her co-workers with the entirely well-meaning intention of easing the path of the World Teacher.

Your reviewer was present in the huge tent holding AB and over 3,000 people on that fateful morning, 3 August 1929, and he well remembers K's resonant voice, needing no microphone, ringing out for everyone to hear his determination to dissolve the Order of the Star, as he happened to be its head:

> 'I maintain that Truth is a pathless land . . . Truth, being limitless, unconditioned, unapproachable by any path whatsoever, cannot be organized; nor should any organization be formed to lead or coerce people along any particular path . . . an organization becomes a crutch . . . prevents the individual from growing, from establishing his uniqueness, which lies in the discovery for himself of that absolute unconditioned Truth . . . My only concern is to set men unconditionally and absolutely free' (pp. 75–9).

I remember the exhilaration and exaltation I felt, similar to but far more intense than that felt four years previously when I heard Klemperer conduct Beethoven's Ninth Symphony in Berlin.

In 1930 K resigned from the TS. AB died in 1933, CWL in 1934. K had healing powers. He helped Aldous Huxley (p. 84) with his blindness and cured Vimla Thakkar (pp. 204–6) of her deafness. He also helped Nitya and Ghanashyam Mehta with their eyesight. Besides having psychical gifts, K had mystical experiences, apart from 'the Process', between the end of May and 20 June 1948, in Ootacamund (pp. 125–30). It was here Prime Minister Nehru sought an interview and asked K, 'Tell me what is right action and what is right thought.' After a more than three-minute silence K spoke slowly, 'Right action is only possible when the mind is silent and there is a seeing of *what is*.'

Many people have declared that K was beautiful. P quotes Bernard Shaw's words (p. 81) to Hesketh Pearson that K was the most beautiful human being he had ever seen. When Fritjof Capra visited me after a conference of scientists at Brockwood Park, he repeated several times, 'But he is so beautiful.' K's charming courtesy and considerateness and his impeccable manners endeared him to everybody. Where necessary, he also told you the truth gently (as the Buddha did to Ambattha), but with flashing eyes.

K freely shared with others what he had. As a boy he often came home minus slate or pencil or book (—some lad hadn't one!); grown up, he shared his own good clothes with his friends. K nursed bedridden Nitya in every way during his last illness in Ojai. He never lost his temper (p. 84) or reacted against anyone who was impatient with him; he easily forgot wrong done to him; he met all violence or opposition with a gentle silence that healed; he was all-understanding, all-loving.

Such was K, the man, whose passion for Truth when answering the question 'What is God?', included the following words (p. 192):

> 'To find out what God—Truth is, one has to understand sorrow, and the struggle of human existence. To go beyond the mind there must be a cessation of the self, the "me". It is only then, that which we all worship, seek, comes into being.'

K spent nearly eight years in isolation during World War II in Ojai. The U.S. draft board heard his views on why he could not fight, or join an army. They let him stay as there was no transport available to return him to India, but forbade him to give talks; he had to report to the police regularly.

> 'He walked for endless miles spending whole days in the wilderness, alone, forgetful of food, listening and

> observing . . . meeting wild bears and rattlesnakes, facing them without movement of body and mind. The wild beast would pause, its cautious watchful eyes meeting K's silent eyes for several minutes; the animal sensing a total absence of fear, would turn and move away' (p. 85).

K lived in a sparsely furnished log cabin; woke up early; had a long walk, cooked breakfast, washed up and cleaned the cabin. He played the Ninth Symphony of Beethoven (the only record he had) every day, listening, meditating (p. 80). He also experimented (p. 87) with yogic austerities—fasting for days, being silent, breathing (see the *Mahāsīhanāda Sutta*, M.1.77–81, for the Buddha's ascetic practice), but he dismissed these yogic stances as play, peripheral and of no account.

On p. 88 there is a delightful story of a picnic with Aldous and Maria Huxley, Greta Garbo, Charlie Chaplin and Paulette Goddard, Bertrand Russell and Christopher Isherwood. Read it. You will laugh. K himself laughed a great deal, like some Buddhist monks do.

Like Plato, K mainly used the dialogue form through which to convey his insights and to answer questions. The Socratic Dialogue is a logical, rational form. If Socrates saw that the answer to his question was wrong or inadequate, he would argue the problem in such a way as to bring about a confession from the other person that he was mistaken. K's way was different. He never took the 'you are wrong, I am right' stance. Instead of giving a direct answer to the problem, he would say something suggestive, perhaps follow it up with more suggestive statements and awaken the other person's mind so that the *person himself understood* the problem or question. In that understanding the answer lay hidden and it would be the right answer for that particular person. K's concern was not to reel off a bright answer—Q.E.D.—but to stir the questioner's own intelligence into action.

K used silences, sometimes long silences, between his sentences. It seems that, being very sensitive psychically, he was aware whether the other person's mind was stirring aright or not. So he would continue with suggestive and deeply meaningful statements till he felt that the person, or the audience, was rhythmically counterpointing in harmony with his own insight. A newcomer would probably find some of his statements incomprehensible. For instance: 'the observer is the observed'; 'for there to be life, there must be death'; 'thinker and thought are not separate, for if thought is removed where is the thinker?'; 'thought is material'.

Parts 2 to 5 of the book are a *tour de force* of P's special ability to blend K's dialogue-discussion-discourse with his life. K's teaching is often very difficult to comprehend—e.g. chapters like numbers 10, 15, 24, 25, practically the whole of Part 6 of the book, especially chapters 39, 40, 42 and 45. But I found that by re-reading each difficult passage several times, quite slowly, light arose. K's vision, understanding and expression often defeat intellectual grasping. Perhaps their very clarity and simplicity elude our conditioned brain—we can look with delight at the full moon, whereas we can endure the mid-day sun only for a flashing moment or two.

Our training in school and university conditions us to look for what we call a rational presentation in a logical framework in the Western European sense that derives from Plato and Aristotle. But the realized Truth of the seer or prophet happens to by-pass this logic and rationality. It is a-logical and a-rational. Logic and the illogical, rationality and irrationality are integrated and transcended. They become a holistic otherness, for which concept and word (thought and language) are inadequate media of expression or communication. The mystery works in silence and its mode of working is unknowable, even as fertilization in the plant and animal worlds is a mystery, or the spontaneous uprising of liking or dislike between two strangers at their first meeting is a mystery.

And yet, despite the inefficiency of concept or word to convey profundity, concept and word can produce a thrill, pristine and intensely alive, which, in course of time, may bear a not inadequate, not misleading interpretation and understanding. It may be somewhat like a photograph you glimpsed last year which enables you to recognize the living person if perchance you meet him unexpectedly.

At lunchtime in Ojai on his 85th birthday, K said: 'If I knew the Buddha would be speaking here tomorrow, nothing in the world could stop me from going to listen to him. And I would follow him to the very end.' It would be well for all of us to take those words to heart. (They occur in Asit Chandmal's book *One Thousand Moons*, p. 19.)

In 1931 Indira Nehru (afterwards Gandhi) and P first met as teenagers, at Anand Bhavan, the family home of the Nehrus in Allahabad. They became friends in 1955 after P came to live in Delhi (p. 355). P often spoke of K to Indira, who had read Huxley's *Doors of Perception*. Indira became Prime Minister of India in 1966 and first met K at dinner in P's house in the late '50s. In the autumn of 1976, when the situation in India was fraught with difficulty and led to the Emergency which roused much opposition to her, Indira sought K's advice and then decided to release all detainees and call for elections. She lost. The Janata Government stepped in, but soon broke down. Elections in 1979 returned her with an overwhelming majority. Shortly afterwards, K told P that Indira would face great sorrow in the year to come. As fate would have it, her elder son Sanjay was killed in an air crash. In December 1980 she, together with her family—Rajiv and Sonia and young Rahul and Prihanka—visited K at his school in Rishi Valley. During her eighteen hours there, P writes (p. 353), 'an unwavering compassion flowed from K, enveloping her'. She returned to Delhi, reinvigorated, and there was an exchange of letters with K. But her life was moving swiftly towards its destiny. Trouble in Punjab blew up, climaxing in the occupation by troops of the Golden Temple of the Sikhs in Amritsar. In revenge, on 31 October 1984, two of her own Sikh security guards shot Indira as she walked from her residence to her office. She fell, mortally wounded, was rushed to hospital, and died within hours.

I found Part 6 of the book difficult. Sometimes beyond my grasp, at others peculiarly elusive, but always revealing if re-read slowly in quietude. Usually, I do not care for biographies, for how can the conditioned brain of the biographer accurately present the whole truth about any person? But this biography made me feel I was with K in his travels, with his talks, seeing some of his revelations.

It is a great book, a good book. It leaves one a better being for having read it—and I have read the whole of it three times and some of the elusive sections four or five times.

Can we sum up teaching which is whole, the Light of Infinity and Eternity? It is itself the No-Thing/Everything, the All without beginning or ending, the Mystery/Paradox which transcends itself and remains itself. Can *we* sip the morning dew sipped up by the sun? Revealed Truth is Unrevealed Fact. Only by the death of all limitation, only in still silence, shall we know that limitless love, that wordless wisdom, that thought-less Truth which for a little time and in a special place we named Krishnaji, a whisper that fills Eternity.

P is an artist as a writer: 'In secret conclave, they (the ancient seers) kept alive and resonant the petals of a perennial wisdom' (p. 149). 'October is a tender month in Delhi. The damp heat wanes and morning dew ushers in the winter. Warm shawls emerge from clove-scented wrappers, and festivals celebrate the harvests of the fields of the vast countryside' (p. 363).

But her finest artistry is embodied in the very end of the book (p. 501). The place is Pine Cottage, Ojai. The day is 16 February 1986. Krishnaji lies dying:

> I saw Krishnaji around one o'clock on the day of my departure on February 16. I sat with him for some time. He was in great pain, but his mind was clear and lucid. I said I would not say good-bye for there would be no separation. With great effort, he lifted my hand to his lips. The grip was still firm. He lay cradled in a silence which enveloped me. As I was leaving, he said, 'Pupul, tonight I shall go for a long walk in the high mountains. The mists are rising.' I left his room without turning back.
>
> That night, at nine o'clock Pacific Standard Time, Krishnaji slept, to start his long walk into the high mountains. The mists were rising, but he walked through the mists and he walked away.

We owe, and it is our happy fortune to owe, a debt of deep gratitude to this biographer.

Namaste! Pupul Jayakar. And when it is your turn to enter into that vast and glorious night, may you blissfully walk away as he walked away.

Living the Good Life

Interviews with Phiroz Mehta by John Snelling

(1986)

Part One: The Formative Years

J.S.: *Phiroz, could we begin with your early years in Ceylon [Sri Lanka]: how did religion affect your life then?*
P.M.: I was brought up as a Zarathushtrian because both my parents were Parsis, but I went to a school where there were boys of various different religions and I naturally got interested in talking with them. Also in school we had assembly like you have in England, and Christianity was rammed down our throats there. I was always interested in deeply religious matters, particularly in the meaning of immortality: whence did we come and whither do we go after death? Later on we had a Theosophical friend in our family who used to come and see us, and I got very attracted to the idea of the unity of religions as far as the fundamentals are concerned. That was how I came to read about other religions and to study them and practise meditation.
J.S.: *Was there any experience of religious insight when you were young—or did your interest just rest upon a feeling, perhaps?*
P.M.: I think it was more a feeling. The ideas which I came across about death, rebirth and the after-death state showed me the necessity of living the good life, but I had nothing that you could call a mystical experience during my childhood.

J.S.: *Did you meet anyone who seemed to embody anything special in the religious line?*
P.M.: Besides some of the leaders of the Theosophical Society, I didn't meet anybody particularly inspiring. I did meet two or three Christian missionaries and I used to have long arguments with them. I was very argumentative as a child and used to drive them frantic!
J.S.: *They didn't expect you to debate with them?*
P.M.: Quite! They adopted the attitude, 'We *know*; we belong to the true faith and have come to save your heathen souls.' I showed them that all that was quite non-sensical.
J.S.: *Even then?*
P.M.: Oh, yes. I had the ability to discuss things and argue just like a barrister.
J.S.: *You were a Zarathushtrian, you said.*
P.M.: That's right. The name of the ancient Iranian Prophet was *Zarathushtra*, but the Greeks hellenized it to *Zoroastrēs* (as used by Plato, for example), which was modified to *Zoroaster*. The religion became *Zoroastrianism*, and remains so for most people to this day, though I prefer the old Iranian names: *Zarathushtra* and *Zarathushtrianism*.
J.S.: *How was this religion celebrated in Ceylon when you were a boy?*
P.M.: Occasionally we had a prayer festival, a *Jasan*, (originally *Jashn*). Zarathushtrians would gather together and the priest recited Avestan prayers for about an hour or so. At this ceremony a good deal of food was consecrated, mainly fruit, together with some very pleasant preparations made from semolina, flour and so on. Each of the participants said his own chosen prayers out of a big prayer book; there was no congregational worship as in Christianity; the prayers were not said in unison. Then afterwards we all stood round a table and enjoyed the consecrated food. In addition, we also had our initiation ceremonies, which corresponded broadly to the Christian confirmation ceremony. I don't remember having any special baptismal ceremony as such in early childhood, but the initiation ceremony was usually carried out somewhere between one's seventh and twelfth years.
J.S.: *Did you debate with the Zarathushtrian priests?*

P.M.: No, only with the Christian missionaries. I had by the time I was 12 years old read a good deal about Hinduism and Buddhism as well as what we Parsis were ourselves taught. I debated with them on those grounds. Of course in those days I believed implicitly in the main Buddhist and Hindu teachings.

J.S.: *You came across both Hinduism and Buddhism in Ceylon?*

P.M.: Oh, yes—in fact all the religions, for all were represented in my school, except perhaps Sikhism and Jainism.

J.S.: *Was Zarathushtrianism free of the dogmatic element: that it was the only true religion?*

P.M.: I think so, very largely. Of course, most Zarathushtrians believe it is the *best* religion, and the later scriptures call it that; but this seems to be a universal characteristic of all the religions: 'Other religions do have some good things, of course, but ours is the best'! But I myself felt free to study other religions and in fact my mother encouraged me to do so.

J.S.: *How did you first come across Buddhism?*

P.M.: Just by reading books. Then I noticed that it differed substantially from Hinduism, which had, for instance, the notion of a personal entity, the *jivātman*, which comes back into incarnation life after life until final liberation is attained; whereas Buddhism, of course, has no such thing as an *ātman* in its teachings. I noticed that very carefully and couldn't reconcile the two views at all.

Also the Governor of Ceylon when I was a boy was Sir Robert (later Lord) Chalmers. He was a Pali Scholar and very sympathetic to Buddhism. He came one day to my school and spent quite a lot of time with my class making inquiries as to what the boys knew of Buddhism. That was his main interest. There might have been some slight conversation on that occasion, but I can't remember anything. Then on another occasion, going home from school on my bicycle, I found myself travelling in the same direction as him and, being very young and afraid of no-one, I rode beside his carriage and I think we exchanged a few words of greeting.

J.S.: *What school did you attend?*

P.M.: I started at the Government Training College in Colombo, a secondary school of a very high standard that was later amalgamated with the Royal College. This took us up to the Cambridge Junior and Senior, the London Matriculation and the London Intermediate Science examinations; then, if we did really well, we won a scholarship to Oxford or Cambridge.

J.S.: *Did you win such a scholarship?*

P.M.: No, although I did come first in Chemistry, I didn't, because I had no birth certificate. You see, I was born in Cambay [now in Gujurat state, about 300 miles north of Bombay] and there was no such thing there, the date of birth accepted by everyone being that of one's horoscope.

J.S.: *I have the impression that generally your early life was a happy one; that you belonged to a happy family?*

P.M.: Yes, I think so on the whole. My father was the Chief Superintendent at the Ceylon Wharfage Company, the biggest landing and shipping concern in Colombo, which was headed by Sir James Lisle-McKay, who later became Lord Inchcape. He wanted someone reliable and efficient to run it for him and he found that person in my father, who served him for about forty-two years.

J.S.: *Did you have any brothers or sisters?*

P.M.: One sister, who's now World President of the International Planned Parenthood Federation. She studied for the Bar and was, I think, the youngest woman to pass her exams in London. There was a tendency in the family for the children to become barristers as my father's cousin was Sir Phirozeshah Mehta, who was in his day one of the two foremost barristers in all India (the other was Motilal Nehru, father of Jawaharlal). My father, noticing that I was such an argumentative child, thought I'd make a barrister. I did in fact join Gray's Inn and studied Law when I eventually came to Cambridge, in addition to my other work there. I passed in Criminal Law but I was very disturbed by the ethical side. You may have done wrong but, if your barrister was clever enough, he could get you off scot-free. Where then is justice? This troubled me.

J.S.: *You had a disposition towards science, I believe?*

P.M.: Yes, yes—particularly Chemistry. That started in 1912, when I saw the first experiments demonstrated by the Chemistry teacher. They so fascinated me, particularly seeing things like iron wire burning in a jar of oxygen. It just happened by chance that I was very good at Chemistry, never getting less than 90 or 92 per cent in examinations.

J.S.: *This was in fact what you studied in Cambridge?*

P.M.: Yes, I did Natural Sciences, though I fell ill in my third year and couldn't sit the greater part of my exams, so I didn't even get an aegrotat degree. Twenty six years later, however, when I had ten weeks to spare from lecturing work, I crammed all that was necessary and got through then. My subject was not Natural Sciences for this exam, it was History.

J.S.: *In Cambridge you met Christmas Humphreys at the Theosophical Society, I believe. Can you remember your first encounter with him?*

P.M.: No, not the first encounter; but I do remember how amusing he used to be. For instance, he was once describing the rooms of one of our people and he said, 'Wonderful rugs and curtains and some very nice chairs, a gramophone and *millions* of records.' T.C.H. had that wonderful voice of his and made you laugh at such things!

J.S.: *Never prone to understatement?*

P.M.: No!

J.S.: *What impact did Cambridge make upon you?*

P.M.: I loved it right from the beginning, both the academic and the social sides. I was accepted by the other undergraduates and made friends easily. That was particularly due to my music. An Indian who could play Beethoven sonatas, Chopin and Lizst on the piano!—that gave me an easy entrée everywhere.

J.S.: *Did you start the piano at an early age?*

P.M.: In my kindergarten days. But then when I was about eleven or twelve, I just stopped. I'd got to dislike it because I'd been made to practise so much. And then one fine day I happened to read a list of the great Western musicians in some book and at the same time came across one of Mendelssohn's *Songs Without Words*, which is a very beautiful piece of music; these things drew me back to the piano.

J.S.: *Did music and science ever eclipse religion in your life?*

P.M.: No, religion played the greater part in my life always.

J.S.: *But at Cambridge you must have been out of touch with Zarathushtrians. Did you attend Chapel?*

P.M.: No, never. I had no need to, for by that time I was conversant with all the religions and believed in living the good life, the religious life, the ethical life. That was all that interested me. Rituals and ceremonies never presented any attraction.

J.S.: *You saw, then, the basic practice as being one of* sīla *or ethical conduct?*

P.M.: Exactly. To live the good life and be a good human being.

J.S.: *How does this foster the development of wisdom or insight?*

P.M.: It doesn't at that young age, especially in a person of my temperament. You see, by the time I was a young man I had read a great deal, not only concerning the religions of the world but in Eastern and Western Philosophy as well. Plato I had first read when I was ten (in translation, of course!); also a biological work of Aristotle. My father had a good library, including the works of some of the German philosophers: Fichte, Schelling, Hegel and Schopenhauer. Later I attended certain courses given in Colombo by an English philosopher named W. D. Stace, who was of some note and expounded Greek and European Philosophy very well. All that thrilled me very much. I was a little conceited!

J.S.: *Did you practise any form of meditation at that time?*

P.M.: Yes, a sort of meditation—the primary stages, you know, which are to be found in both Hinduism and Buddhism; but it didn't lead very far at the time. I don't know why not.

J.S.: *Following Cambridge, I suppose you embarked upon a career?*

P.M.: Yes, I studied under Solomon, the great pianist, for 8 ½ years. I gave one or two little recitals here and there but nothing great until in 1934 I went to India and gave my first public recital in Lahore. Sir Robert Emerson was Governor of the Punjab at the time and gave his patronage. Of course, the whole of the British community turned up as well as a good few Indians, because this was the first time that any Indian had given a pianoforte recital entirely on his own. I returned to England in 1935 but then went back to India again in 1938, when I met Silvia, daughter of Dr J. H. Shaxby, on board ship. We were married in England in July 1939. When World War II broke out, I applied to join the R.A.F. Three doctors examined me for fitness and the principal one eventually said: 'Mr Mehta, the report on your physical condition is C.3, so we won't trouble you at all.' He had such a benign expression on his face as he said it!

J.S.: *You weren't very strong at that time?*

P.M.: That's so. What happened was that by Christmas 1940 all important sources of vitamins for us vegetarians, and other necessary foods, had become rather scarce or even unavailable. I contracted severe neuritis, which lasted five years.

J.S.: *If the R.A.F. was out, what other vocation did you find for yourself?*

P.M.: Lecturing. My father-in-law's very close friend was John Fleure, Professor of Geography in Manchester University. Shortly after Silvia and I were married he visited my father-in-law's house in Cardiff, where we were then living, and suggested that I might be usefully employed writing and lecturing on Indian culture and philosophy. He therefore got a group of people in Manchester University who were holding an extramural conference to invite me to give a lecture on the theme of *Race, Religion and Politics in India*. This was at the end of 1942. Now, I could have spoken on religion alone, but of race and politics I knew very little; so at first I declined the invitation. Then something got into me and I said, 'I'll have a go . . .' So I came to London, picked several books from the India House Library, studied them carefully and prepared my lecture. By good luck it was very much appreciated by both the audience and the other speakers, who included Miss I. B. Horner. She had a little conference with her fellow speakers after the lecture and they decided they'd ask me if I'd be willing to lecture to troops on Indian subjects. You see, the War Office had an Education Department at the time. I said, 'Yes, I'll do that,' since my first lecture had been so well appreciated. That's how my lecturing work started. Inside three months I was lecturing every day of the week, by request, giving in all hundreds of lectures during the war years. After the War the lecture service was closed by the Conservative Government and I was without a job, apart from having a few piano pupils.

Part Two: Deepening Insight

P.M.: At our Reunion Dinner at Trinity College in 1954, a friend suggested to me that I teach in schools as I had a Master's degree. He gave me some letters of introduction and that began my schoolteaching career. In later years I confined myself to Chemistry because that was the subject I knew really well.

J.S.: *Did you like teaching children?*

P.M.: I loved it! My last five years teaching in London were the happiest of my teaching life, because then I taught more or less only fifth and sixth form classes. Some of the sixth formers were magnificent students!

J.S.: *To return to the religious side of things: did you ever have a teacher or belong to a group?*

P.M.: No, I never had a special guru or any such thing. It was all my own study, my own practice, my own observation. That is how I have now come to talk and lecture on the topic of holistic consciousness: that the evolution of consciousness culminates in an all-inclusive consciousness that functions in the context of the infinite and the eternal. As far as I am aware, this topic has not yet been adequately expounded by theologians and philosophers.

J.S.: *How did this develop? Can you describe the process?*

P.M.: That's very difficult. I do, however, remember the date when something significant happened because it made such a difference afterwards. On the night of 22 February 1952, for hours and hours I was in a very quiet state, and suddenly it happened: *I realized the meaning of the silence.* It all came quite suddenly and from that time onwards my understanding of the whole matter naturally changed steadily. Then in 1978 I saw that the context of Transcendence—that is Transcendence relative to us as we are—was the infinite and the eternal, and that the truly great spiritual teachers ('the perfected holy ones', to use the Buddha's phrase) were able to function in terms of it. They were at home in the infinite and the eternal, and understood what holistic consciousness meant; they were also at home in the context of the temporal and the finite.

That is, they were equally at home in *both* the mortal and the immortal contexts. According to circumstance, they could function in the context of holistic consciousness, or, when required, in the ordinary human context, but then with the perfect and purifying influence of holistic consciousness still at play.

J.S.: *Krishnamurti maintains that the ability to function from the higher level of consciousness actually transforms the cells of the brain.*

P.M.: I wouldn't be at all surprised if that is true. As you know, our brains bear the evidence of some 600,000,000 years of evolution, proceeding through the reptilian phase to that of the mammals, the primates and now us humans.

J.S.: *Was the initial insight preceded by anything significant, such as a trauma of some sort?*

P.M.: No, no trauma as such. Actually it happened after I had been giving a lecture, I think in the town of Poole. Somehow or other after I'd got into bed I felt remarkably quiet and peaceful. At around 2 or 3 o'clock in the early morning this intense quietness suddenly inspired me with the significance of the silence and I realized that one of the essential things in connection with this silence was that all discursive thinking stops. *The brain stops talking*—that's what it amounts to.

J.S.: *The perennial riddle, of course, is how people are to achieve this sort of thing for themselves, isn't it? It's always said that it can't be achieved by being pursued.*

P.M.: That is the great thing. You see, people *will* say, I *must* find God'; so I say to them, 'Go and find space,' and they say, 'We *are* in space!'; so then I say, 'Similarly, you will find God, for you *are* in God in that same way! It is not so much *you* that will find God as God will find you. It is not the person, the existential human being, that realizes the Supreme; it is the Transcendent that realizes *Itself* as the perfect human through the existential human being. *All you have to do is be silent.*'

J.S.: *Then it's like an action from the other side?*

P.M.: Exactly! If the One Total Reality is the supreme thing—the manifestation of the Absolute, if you like—then it is the Absolute that is working through everything that is. So all that is here has emerged out of THAT, which I personally like to call the Primordial

Undifferentiated Creative Energy holding in itself the potentiality of everything that has emerged. It is THAT which realizes itself as the perfect flower through the rose or the gardenia or whatever, as the perfect gem through the diamond and the sapphire, and similarly it realizes *Itself* as the perfect human through mankind.

J.S.: *Why has discursive thought arisen if it is such an impediment?*

P.M.: It is not so much a question *why* but *how* it has arisen. This is how it seems to me:

This Primordial Creative Energy, by means of self-constriction, goes through various grades of manifestation and being until it reaches the most concrete expression of itself: solid matter. Then comes, so to say, the return journey. If the first part is the *in*volution process, then this is the *e*volution process—evolution not only in the organic sense, but in the spiritual sense too. Consciousness, which became absolutely locked up in the mineral, begins to open out again. This manifest world is the apparatus through which consciousness works and releases itself from all the impediments to which the apparatus is subject. In the human kingdom, we come to the stage when we can talk, when the brain cells can retain impressions and the senses are functioning and so forth; and so the process of discursive thinking comes into operation.

Consciousness in itself is that aspect of Transcendence which is *all-knowingness*. We know what 'being conscious of' means: if I look there, I see a fireplace with a stove giving heat, so I become conscious of that thing. But what is consciousness itself? It is indescribable, but it is that which is working through everything. Was it Rūmī, the Sufi sage, who said, 'I was mineral; I became plant; I became animal; and now I am a man'? In the *Golden Verses of Pythagoras* you also come across the statement, 'When thou arrivest at the most pure Aether thou shalt be an immortal god.' But, of course, this existential organism will never be immortal. In all likelihood, however, matter may begin to disappear as and when consciousness moves through those subtler and subtler grades of being. What you and I call *spirit* is, for us, the most subtle expression of the Primordial Creative Energy; what we call *matter* is the most concrete expression of it. And it is between these two poles that the cycle of involution/evolution takes place.

J.S.: *Isn't there a danger here of creating a kind of warring duality between matter and spirit? There is a saying by the Catholic thinker, Eric Gill, to the effect that man is both flesh and spirit, both made by God, both good. Yet the general tendency is to think that spirit is good and matter bad.*

P.M.: This unfortunate way of thinking only came about in recent millennia.

J.S.: *For a long time people seem to have been lacerating themselves for having physical bodies. And many women seem to feel that things like the persecution of the witches represent the victimization of matter by spirit.*

P.M.: I think these are all mistakes. That is why I have always used the phrase, 'One Total Reality'. This is all-inclusive, you see; each has its place. To use an analogy: We know something about electrical energy, but electrical energy itself needs an apparatus through which it can function. So, if we have a bulb and electrical energy flows through it, then the bulb will give light. It's like that, though that is still to talk in terms of a separation between the apparatus and the energy. In the case of the Totality, however, this Primordial Creative Energy itself becomes its own container, its own apparatus (i.e. matter and the manifested universe), and in so doing consciousness becomes constricted all along the line. When it becomes matter, then the material world becomes the apparatus through which this consciousness will once again release itself. Consciousness is not, of course, *my* consciousness, or indeed anybody's consciousness; it is just consciousness—the Totality.

J.S.: *You seem to be saying that spirit and matter are mutally interdependent and ultimately the same, as in the Nirvana-Saṃsāra correlation. There has been, though, particularly in the West, the notion that the spirit can somehow rise to some pure, free place beyond matter.*

P.M.: It is admitted that the spirit is infinite and eternal. If that is so, can you split it up? For instance, the only thing that we ordinarily experience as infinite is space: it contains everything. Now, can you cut off slabs of space and appropriate any one slab for yourself? So too, you can't say, 'This is *my* spirit; this is *my* immortal soul'; there is no entity like that which is a separate thing. *I say that the whole of the Primordial Creative Energy, the whole of eternity, the whole of infinity is totally embodied in every single manifestation which makes up the cosmos of which we are conscious in separative terms.* This *separativeness* is the great trouble; through it arises the idea of self and not-self, and that idea is the root of all sin and all suffering and all misery. The real *dukkha* is our awareness of existence in terms of self and not-self, as two separate things. From this arises the conflict that urges man to *conquer* Nature, as he puts it, which is nonsensical and incredibly stupid—at least it is so to me, though I may of course be wrong!

J.S.: *Ken Wilber, writing in* The Middle Way,* *once put in a good word for the 'I', the ego, which comes in for a very bad press in spiritual circles. He pointed out that it is a necessary stage.*

P.M.: The separate 'I' *is* a necessary stage; you can't bypass it. But it is also the source of all conflict. The whole process of development and fruition ultimately enables the person to become free of isolative and separative self-consciousness. And this is where the ethical life comes in. It is the greatest power for freeing the individual from the sense of separation, because it is one thing to have the ideal that *All Life is One* and quite another to become fully conscious of it. A thought, after all, is only a string of words. What potency has it? It is but the shadow of the truth. It can help, though. It can be a starting point: the baby stage, so to speak. Then, as we grow inwardly, we become conscious of the reality that the thought is trying to represent. When you're really *conscious* of something, that something expresses itself in all your thought and feeling, your speech and action. That is the fruition which Transcendence itself realizes as perfect humanity.

J.S.: *Today, there is often a tendency to become preoccupied with techniques that are thought to hasten the process of insight and to overlook the* sīla *side, the ethical side, don't you think?*

P.M.: Look, when I was born I never sought any technique that would allow me to grow. I just grew up, didn't I? I mean, I could not predetermine how the organism should grow. It's the same with the whole process of being.

J.S.: *So the spiritual life is a natural unfolding that doesn't need any special aids to hasten it?*

**In Praise of Ego: An Uncommon Buddhist Sermon*, Vol. 58, pp. 151 ff.

P.M.: Yes. And just as wrong living in the matter of eating and drinking produces illness or otherwise obstructs the real fruition of the organism, similarly all our desires and passions, fears and beliefs also obstruct our fruition. The purification of the psyche empties the whole of the psyche of its rigid beliefs, misconceptions, etc. Now, I know that Krishnamurti always says that meditation is the emptying of the content of consciousness, and I believe that there he is using 'consciousness' in the same sense as I use 'psyche'. It is, in fact, not the consciousness but the psyche that is emptied or made void by seeing through the insubstantiality of all thoughts, feelings, perceptions and so forth. The *Diamond Sutra* is marvellous on this subject. If we see through all that and empty the psyche, then there is no obstruction to the light of Transcendence shining freely through the existential being. Then the brain itself will become the instrument by which insights and profound ideas may emerge that can help others onward.

J.S.: *So you don't personally advocate meditation techniques?*

P.M.: I don't practise anything like that any more.

J.S.: *Such techniques certainly seem to have a profound effect upon people—at least in the short term.*

P.M.: They certainly do have effects and people mistake those effects, which are ephemeral, for the real thing.

J.S.: *They can also be energizing . . .*

P.M.: Oh, yes, they can energize too. But, you see, even great saints have been known to fall. The real technique, if you can call it a technique, is summed up in *sammā sati* and *sammā samadhi*. Jesus also said, 'Watch and pray', which to me is identical. You have to be watchful, aware, awake. Note how often the Buddha said, 'I am the Wake, the Awakened One.' What does that mean? He uses the term 'I' innumerable times, so it is not the destruction of the 'I', the ego, which is the main task. Far from it. The perfecting of the 'I', the ego—that is to say, the microcosmic individual—is required of us. This allows the consciousness to reach the holistic stage, where it becomes inclusive of the Totality, and the macrocosmic individuality is manifested through the microcosmic individuality. This is how I see things, though I don't claim any finality for my view.

Part Three: Let Be What Is

J.S.: *One does seem to encounter, through one's attempts to live the spiritual life, the dark side of oneself. I think a lot of people find that hard to handle.*

P.M.: I'm not really very much in favour of the expression, 'the dark side of oneself'. The existential being is a single whole. *Let be what is.* Keep on doing the right thing, as far as one can know what the right thing to do is, and what is troublesome will cease of itself to be troublesome. All storms come to an end, sooner or later, so one must realize that and be content with what one actually is, and *tend* what one is so that it can really flower by its own self. That will bring out the uniqueness of the individual being. That is very important, because Transcendence itself, Creative Energy, is endlessly varied. Its originality in producing the new is something quite extraordinary. To me, every single human being is unique in his or her own way: has within him- or herself divine potentialities. Just let them come to fruition.

J.S.: *In the West we seem to have a tradition of wanting to be good and being proud of what virtues we possess, but, on the other hand, trying to repress or annihilate anything in ourselves that is bad or weak.*

P.M.: That is true. You know, there are those who use the phrase: *'Don't struggle hard. Leave it to God.'* There's a great deal of wisdom in that, you know! Just leave it to that which is transcendent and the Transcendent will do the needful, provided you have the good sense to let It do so. We also have statements like: *'If you take one step towards the Divine, the Divine moves leagues towards you.'* That is a fact because we are so completely interrelated and interactive with the Totality that whatever we do produces a response from Totality. This is the deep meaning of *karma. Karma* is derived from the root, *kri*. Of course, the dictionaries will tell you that it means *to do* or *to make*; but those are poor definitions. To me, the root *kri* fundamentally means *creative action*. This creative action is eternal and infinite.

J.S.: *So you are saying that the Ultimate really wants to work through us and is trying to do so?*
P.M.: Yes and no. The Ultimate—I prefer to call it Totality—isn't trying. It just waits for us to make the first move. Then it necessarily and inevitably makes a response.
J.S.: *The question comes up now and again whether this Totality is indifferent to man, or whether it cares about his fate.*
P.M.: These are incorrect ways of expressing the matter. You see, whenever we talk like that, as, for instance, the theists do when they say, 'God cares for us and wants us to do so-and-so,' then it is all nonsensical talk. Talking in theistic language has great limitations, for the God cited is invariably a creation of the human brain. You'll find that all the God-conceptions of the world are all human beings apotheosized.
J.S.: *Is it then possible to say anything about Ultimate Reality—or are all such attempts futile?*
P.M.: It defies description. All description is necessarily limiting, because all language represents the sphere of the finite, temporal and mortal. Since we are ourselves existential beings, let us be content with tending the existential in the right way so that it is sane and healthy, and naturally and spontaneously does the right thing. But it mustn't strive for *itself*: '*I* want to reach Nirvana; *I* want to find God; *I* want to be a Buddha; *I* want to be a yogi.' All that is egotistic nonsense! One might as well say, 'I want to be Shakespeare.' If a fellow is endowed with little mastery over language and lacks Shakespeare's remarkable insights, he's talking nonsense if he says that. I discovered the truth of this partly through my own personal experience. When I took to music, I wanted to be the greatest pianist in the world. But nothing of that sort happened—and it couldn't happen. What I discovered was that I simply didn't have the gift to reach that stage—I just did not have it in me. And where composing music was concerned, I had no real sense of harmony or counterpoint or fugue, or anything like that. To this day, if you gave me a tune, I couldn't harmonize it; I couldn't write a simple accompaniment. So it was somewhere in the late Fifties that I really discovered that it was not my vocation at all. Then, very fortunately, writing and lecturing on religious topics arose. Adding all that to

the experience I had in 1952 helped me to know that the limited self is indeed the *limited* self!

J.S.: *What do you think is the distinctive greatness of Buddhism?*

P.M.: The distinctive greatness of the Buddha's Teaching is the supreme emphasis laid upon living the pure, virtuous life and freeing oneself both from all selfness and from the unfortunate misconceptions that had sprung up after the Upanishadic teachings were first given. The Upanishadic teachings really touched both the heights and the depths. Less perceptive minds invented this permanent entity, the *jivātman*, the 'immortal' soul or spirit as presented in the other religions. Thus they spoil the greatness of the teachings. The Buddha, however, drew people's attention to the fact that the existential being, the identifiable separate entity, is necessarily mortal; it is not the Deathless. He used the term *Deathless* and that's one of the remarkable things about the Buddhist presentation: it presents the truth about ourselves in negative terms. For example, we do *not* know LOVE, but we *do* know hate through daily experience. We can only deal with what we know. In that way Buddhism is so practical! The Upanishads, on the other hand, had put it thus: '*Neti, neti*' ('Not this, not this'), with regard to the Transcendent. And the Buddha pointed out that the five elements composing the existential being—*rūpa, vedanā, saññā, saṃkhārā* and *viññāṇa*—are all perishable, but are also things that we know and of which we are conscious. People had formerly thought that perhaps *rūpa* is immortal or that *saṃkhārā* or *viññāṇa* are permanent, but the Buddha pointed out that they are not. But he did use the phrase (this is how I see it; I don't know whether Buddhists would agree): '*Viññāṇaṃ anidassanaṃ anantaṃ sabbato pabhaṃ*', which means, 'consciousness that is signless (or characterless), endless (and therefore beginningless), everywhere shining', which to my view was his way of presenting in five words what the Upanishadic teachers had presented in one, viz. *Ātman*, of which they said: 'It is beginningless, endless, birthless, deathless, hungerless, sorrowless, stainless.' See what the Buddha (for instance in the *Ariyapariyesana Sutta*) himself says: 'Seeking the Unborn, the Undying, the Sorrowless, the Stainless'—he used virtually the same words! Then, of course—I don't know if it's the fault of translation or the limitations of expression twenty-five centuries ago—he also says or is supposed to have said: '*I* won the Birthless, the Stainless, the Sorrowless.' That really is not the best way of putting it. *I* don't win anything; the Birthless, the Sorrowless, the Deathless takes me into *Itself*. In the Buddha's case, the separation between THAT and the man himself was wiped away by his great realization.

J.S.: *What about the path that the Buddha himself trod? Did he fully live the ethical life, do you think?*

P.M.: Unquestionably. Also very remarkable is the story told about him going as a child with his father to the great annual ploughing ceremony. There he went and sat under a tree, and it is said that the shadow of the tree did not move and that the child just sat there, wrapped in the first *jhāna*. A *jhāna* is a transcendent state of consciousness as opposed to *viññāṇic* or discriminitive consciousness. *Viññāṇa* means that I become conscious of this or that through the five senses. *Jhāna* is beyond that; and if the Buddha went into that state as a child then there must already have been an inner stirring, an inner development that was known only to himself.

J.S.: *Does this imply some kind of preparation in previous lives, do you think?*

P.M.: There is no such thing as previous or future lives for any identifiable entity.

J.S.: *But surely there must be predetermining factors preceding that kind of remarkable occurrence?*

P.M.: The existential being—that is to say, the organism—comes into existence via a tremendous process of evolution. The brain bears evidence of this vast process, stretching right back to about 600,000,000 years ago, and passing through the stages of the reptiles, the mammals, the primates and man himself. We inherit all this. But when a sperm fertilizes an ovum, there is a rearrangement of the genes in such a way that the person who comes into being is totally different from either parent and from anyone else who ever lived or will live.

J.S.: *But surely nothing is arbitrary? There must be determining factors?*

P.M.: The determining factors are the activities of the physical elements that produce the person. Look at Mozart. He composed at the age of 4. These things don't just happen. This is the Primordial Creative Energy manifesting its real transcendence.

J.S.: *Why does it create a Mozart so rarely?*

P.M.: Ask Transcendence itself that question! It must be rather difficult, but it happens. I know, of course, that there are people who believe rigidly in *karma* as inevitable, absolute consequence. I think they are mistaken, because that rigid attitude allows no room for any elasticity, whereas the Universe does display elasticity in its functioning. There *is* the element of chance. Take, for instance, the case of an atomic bomb falling on a town and killing off a hundred thousand people. Now the rigid-minded person would say, 'That is *karma*'. I say, 'Nonsense. It is not their *karma* at all. It just happened that way . . .' You see, we want to impose our concept of justice on everything: an eye for an eye, a tooth for a tooth, a cat for a cat, and a dog for a dog. This is our short-sighted, ridiculous way of thinking of justice.

J.S.: *So you really believe in a kind of indeterminacy?*

P.M.: Of course. There is definitely indeterminacy.

J.S.: *Logically, I suppose, if the Infinite has infinite possibilities it must be able to transcend any law that mankind cares to frame.*

P.M.: Yes, it can transcend any law. But what we call a 'law' is just a statistical average and that can't cover every contingency.

J.S.: *I must admit that I was a bit bothered when I first heard you counselling people to live the ethical life, because I couldn't help thinking of what the Christians call the 'whited sepulchres': those righteous men who in the Bible are said to have praised the Lord that they weren't sinful like other men. Some sorts of ethics can seem very cold, rigid and self-serving.*

P.M.: Of course.

J.S.: *You really seem to be talking about another sort of ethical living: a warmer and kinder sort.*

P.M.: Yes, with a real love of life, which means the love of the Totality, because the whole of this cosmos is alive—matter is alive.

J.S.: *I remember in one of your books you wrote that you thought the Buddha must have been an exceptionally sensitive person.*

P.M.: Of course. Unless one is an exceptionally sensitive person, how can one devote one's life to healing the suffering of mankind? You can't do it. An ordinary person says, 'It's not my business. What can I do about it?' But here was a universal problem, and the Buddha saw very clearly that, once the psyche is completely purified, all the problems of mankind just become meaningless.

J.S.: *The Buddha afterwards chose to live a monastic form of life.*

P.M.: Yes, because that was the most appropriate form through which his work could proceed with the best results. Nowadays it's different. Of course, if someone feels that the monastic life is his *métier*, yes, of course: enter a monastery. I tell everyone just to be himself and not to either appreciate or depreciate himself. Be what you are. That does not, however, mean that I should go out and murder someone if I have an inclination to murder, and so forth. One mustn't go to absurd lengths. But everybody has something which is lovely and special to them. All right, let me find out what is lovely and special to me; let me tend that and make it flower as my gift to Totality—that is all. And let me not expect anything for myself. In fact, I can say pretty honestly that I know quite well that there is nothing for *me*, the existential being. This organism here will die and all that was embodied in it returns to the original state. What people call the immortal spirit is just the immortal spirit, that's all.

J.S.: *There's nowhere to return to, then?*

P.M.: There's no going back to anywhere. These are all our limited concepts. There is no forwards or backwards where Infinity and Eternity are concerned. There is no up, no down. This is one of the most difficult things to deal with. People want to reduce to the level of logical thought those things that completely transcend logic. The Buddha himself says quite positively in the *Brahmajala Sutra*, 'This is not to be seen through mere logic.' The transcendent context negates the ordinary context in which we function. I'm not suggesting there are two contexts. There is really only one context: the Total Reality. But we, being what we are, are aware of that single context in dualistic terms: in terms of our mortal context of the finite and the temporal, and then we postulate the immortal context of the infinite and the eternal. A person has reason, perhaps even a right, to postulate the latter if, in his own life, something has happened which has made the immortal context true for him: if, in fact, sometime, somewhere, he has been touched by Transcendence.

Part Four: Life is Always Eternal Life

J.S.: *Phiroz, having begun lecturing during the War and taken up schoolteaching afterwards, when did you begin to hold your group meetings?*
P.M.: In 1962. The first was held on 10 February of that year, so we just completed twenty-three years yesterday.
J.S.: *How did the groups come about?*
P.M.: Ven. Paññāvaddho heard me give talks at the Summer School. Now, I used to go to him now and again to learn about Buddhism, and one day he said to me, 'You have an unusual gift for putting things across. You should form a group and particularly help people to understand the background of Buddhism'—meaning thereby the Upanishadic teachings and so forth. The first time he asked me this, I replied, 'But Ven. Paññāvaddho, I know my own incapacity and ignorance only too well. It is true that I can manage to present things, but this gives people a mistaken impression. They think I know a great deal, but in actual fact I do not.' He just smiled; when I saw him a few days later, he asked me the same thing again and I still excused myself. Then, just three or four days before he was due to fly to Thailand, he asked me for a third time, very earnestly; and I thought, 'I'll have to try.' 'Put a little note up in the Buddhist Society that you'd be willing to start a group,' he told me; 'but they must, of course, be willing to come to your house.' I did so and that started it all off. We have had about five or six hundred people at least come to these meetings over the years, and to date I've given 1,114 talks. Not all were recorded, though. During the first eight years no recordings were made, and then people said that they should be started. In those days I really had a gift for talking. It all just poured out. Sometimes really fine phrases came out and I felt that it would be a pity to lose them, so I agreed to recordings being made. Unfortunately that

lovely aesthetic flow of language, which everyone used to say was like poetry, has stopped. Occasionally a fine phrase may still come out—but, of course, it's the heart of the matter that is really important.

J.S.: *When did you start giving your classes at the Buddhist Society Summer School?*

P.M.: Before 1960, if I remember rightly. Rosa Taylor, who died two years ago, saw that this fellow could do something and she knew four or five others who felt the same. So one Saturday morning, the very day after that year's Summer School had started, she asked me and I said, 'All right.' They wanted me to speak again in the afternoon and to that talk some seven or eight people came, and that started the ball rolling.

J.S.: *You've held your own summer schools too, haven't you?*

P.M.: Yes, but I have now stopped them. The old body is not capable of doing so much.

J.S.: *Phiroz, how do you view the modern world: with despair or with optimism?*

P.M.: Neither despair nor optimism. They are both deceivers. This present state is the result of the activity of all the forces that have been at play in the past. This is how it is. So our task is to really see it for what it actually is, and those who have insight and understanding can contribute their energies towards improving it or healing it, as the case may be.

We were talking last time about *karma* and justice and so forth. I think Aristotle gave the best definition of justice in Book V, chapter 2 of his *Nicomachean Ethics*. The gist of what he says is that justice is the practice of *perfect virtue* towards everyone and towards yourself too. Now, what a wonderful thing to have said! It makes me recall the Buddha's statement: 'He who lives without tormenting himself and without tormenting others, lives with a self become *Brahman*, become the Supreme.' I think that definition of justice is really excellent. Our systems of justice are ones of retributive justice: paying out to others for what they have done. But real justice, the real *karmic* process, is a *healing* process: a *making whole*; an activity which moves towards holistic consciousness. If something happens to my liver, I don't go and cut it out and throw it away. Sometimes I may have to according to the lights of modern science, but that, of course, is not true healing.

J.S.: *Retributive justice in fact generates greater pain and suffering, you mean?*

P.M.: Exactly. To heal, on the other hand, is to make whole; to make perfect, healthy. Now, Zarathushtra taught that right at the beginning. The fifth attribute of Ahuramazda is *haurvatāt*, which means health, wholeness, holiness, completeness; and with it is associated *ameretāt*: immortality. But, of course, Zarathushtra never explained that immortality is to be understood and realized here while we are alive.

Zarathushtra was also the first teacher to teach that the evil-doer will suffer Hell for all time after death and that the good-doer will be in Heaven for all time. Now, I ask, 'How is it possible for a limited, finite human being so to live that he produces an infinite consequence?' Quite impossible! These are absurd teachings and I've said so in my book on Zarathushtra.*

J.S.: *Yes, the absolute nature of Heaven and hell used to oppress me a great deal when I was a boy. I always thought that to go to Hell was to be cast out into a kind of limbo or outer darkness. That was eventually cured when I read Spinoza, who argued that God was One Totality and that there couldn't be anything besides God, because that would compromise his completeness. One could extrapolate from that that there couldn't be an extra dimension, an outer darkness, into which the corrupt could be cast forth.*

P.M.: Spinoza was a remarkable philosopher . . . No, to live a good life just from fear of Hell is the wrong way altogether. Fear has never succeeded in making whole, in making holy—never! I think in the past people clung to the notion of Hell as a means of maintaining the social order. You just simply terrified the populace with this thing. Zarathushtra started it and all established religions, even Buddhism, have hells. Perfectly ridiculous nonsense! Finish with the fear of Hell and simply live the pure human life. Human life means the religious life in the true sense, for the sake of the good life. You will find happiness and fruition thereby. People will nevertheless of course say,

*Reviewed in *The Middle Way*, Vol. 60, no. 4 (February 1986).

'Oh, there are thousands who live good lives and they suffer immense sorrow and pain nevertheless,' and they become perplexed. But this is where one has to realize that the universal process has the element of chance in it. If an atomic bomb falls on a hundred thousand people, they haven't *all* done evil things to *deserve* that sort of consequence. It would be absolute nonsense to say so! And the same is true of the other side of the coin: the joys of Heaven. Look at the joys of Heaven as they are portrayed in the *Koran* and in the later Zarathushtrian teachings. Some eighteen to twenty centuries after Zarathushtra's death, Zarathushtrian teachers wrote of the felicities of Heaven, describing the golden thrones with decorated cushions upon which the righteous sit and the special ornaments which the women wear. Sheer nonsense! The Heavens and Hells of the established religions are very much of this earth—earthy, if you like. All such absurdities should be cleaned out.

J.S.: *Regarding the problem of evil: you once told me that you'd discovered both God and the Devil in yourself?*

P.M.: Yes, indeed.

J.S.: *What sort of terms are you on with the other chap?*

P.M.: I'm on very good terms with them both, only now the one is dissolving away into the other, that is all . . . You see, all this concern with the self, either through fear or anxiety or ignorance, as to what will happen to *me* when I'm dead is futile, for there is no *me* when I am dead. When you're dead, you're dead. It is impossible that I shall be aware of myself as Phiroz Mehta in that other state. Look, every night when I go to sleep I'm not aware that I'm Phiroz Mehta while I'm sleeping dreamlessly. There is blissful ignorance of him. When in fact did this consciousness that I-am-I arise in me? At the very earliest, a few months after my birth, because I heard people saying, 'This is my Mum; this is my Dad—you, he, she, it, I . . .'; and so gradually the brain became conditioned to regard this particular organism that bears my name as *I* and the organism that bears another name as *you*. These are conditioned things; they are unreal. And when I wake up in the morning and know that I am Phiroz Mehta, that is just memory brought over from the previous day. If as the result of some accident my memory of myself is gone, then I don't know that 'I-am-I'.

J.S.: *Krishnamurti makes a big point of the fact that the world* *is created afresh every second, only we drag all our baggage from the past into it.*

P.M.: Yes . . . Look, I've put it in *The Heart of Religion* that the pulse of creation is a *life pulse*. In Qabbalistic teaching it is presented as a life-death pulse. Now, I don't use the word 'death', for death in the minds of practically all human beings is inextricably associated with annihilation. There is no annihilation in reality. Life and death, which I prefer to call life/other-life, is the creative pulse of life eternal. Life is really always eternal life but, because we are conscious only in a limited way, we see it as birth and death. But everything changes every split second. What does that change mean? It means the dying of the old state into the new state, which is a new birth. It's there simultaneously, and if you ever get a touch of real awareness of the nature of eternity, you will see that it is mistaken to talk in terms of life and death. That is the result of our present dualistic consciousness. When you really touch eternity, all dualism completely disappears.

J.S.: *The tendency of dualistic consciousness seems to be to postulate a material container and something else that remains when the container passes away.*

P.M.: No, that's a mistake. The Transcendent, the Primordial Creative Energy, creates its own container out of itself. It is not a separate thing. Now, consciousness is evolving all the time. In some of the later Upanishads, the so-called 'minor' Upanishads, the real fact of the matter was stated outright: that absolute consciousness is identical with *ātman*, with *Brahman*. What more do you want? Meditate on that—*really* meditate upon it.

Of course, that raises a really big question straight away: *what is meditation?* All the systems of meditation are in fact *talking rituals*. They're ritualistic procedures of talking to yourself in certain ways. You say, 'May all beings be happy', and then maybe you think of the teacher and send *mettā* and *karunā* to him, to yourself and to those around you, and so on. Breath-counting is also all talking —talking in an airy way! Mind you, it does produce both physical and psychical results; but it is playing with the mortal not the time; it is not the Deathless. When the existential being can enter into a state of perfect stillness and silence, then the true meditation begins.

J.S.: *The traditional accounts of meditation talk in terms of various categories:* jhānas, *four* samāpattis *and so forth, don't they?*
P.M.: Yes; but, you see, all this categorizing was necessary in the old days. I say it is not necessary now.
J.S.: *You would maintain that the* jhānas *are all just mortal states?*
P.M.: They are, because they start and end, don't they?
J.S.: *Just ephemeral states of bliss?*
P.M.: Not necessarily bliss even.
J.S.: *You'd maintain that insight is something else altogether?*
P.M.: It is beyond all that. There's a wonderful saying by the Buddha in the *Majjhima Nikaya*, where he urges his disciples to stride ever onwards until they finally come to what he calls the cessation of all feeling and perception. These are not the feeling and perception that we ordinarily know but their transcendental counterparts: part of another state of being on the way towards whatever is the Supreme. That also stops, so that, as they say in the Upanishads—and St Theresa describes her own experience of it in virtually the identical words—the body is like a log of wood and it seems hardly to breathe at all. When 'I' can be really silent, then Transcendence speaks, and the language of Transcendence is *revelation*. Revelation is an extraordinary state of consciousness beyond all thought and speech. The Upanishadic teachers put it in a beautiful way: 'that from which speech and mind return, not having found'. *Not having found* is important . . .
J.S.: *We are, though, perpetually caught up in agitation and striving.*
P.M.: Exactly—because we want something for ourselves. There is no striving unless something for oneself is desired.
J.S.: *But isn't it part of our primitive, feral inheritance to struggle for existence: to get food, shelter and so forth? I think people will have a problem with giving up all striving because it's so intimately linked with survival.*
P.M.: One doesn't give up all this; one understands it so completely that one goes on working to produce food, shelter, warmth and so forth, but with the wanting for oneself completely phased out. When we say, 'I am hungry', what precisely does that mean? 'I am hungry' in fact means that a process has gone on inside the body:

all the food already eaten has been dealt with. All the elements necessary for the sustenance of the body have been assimilated, the wastes have been eliminated and, as more sustenance is required, then a certain sensation that we call hunger asserts itself. We associate 'I' with the hunger, but really it's just the simple phenomenon of hunger in the organism.

You mentioned a moment ago our primitive feral disposition to struggle for existence. This struggle for existence is necessary for keeping the organism, the 'you' or the 'me', alive. Besides bodily hunger, which everyone feels, there is a spiritual hunger felt by those who are well aware that the mortal organism is but the apparatus for the immortal Transcendent which, by self-constriction, concretizes as the manifested Totality. One of the purposes of human existence is to enable that imprisoned Transcendence to be liberated and function freely through the perfected holy one. In human beings, consciousness undergoes a developmental process, an evolution through religious living culminating in holistic consciousness. In Buddhistic terms, *viññāṇa*—discriminative, analytic, separative and isolative self-consciousness—is transmuted into *viññāṇaṃ anidassanaṃ anantaṃ sabbato pabhaṃ*—consciousness, which is characterless (or signless), endless, everywhere shining. Holistic consciousness is all-embracing and not isolative or separative. It is not restricted to 'I' or 'Mine', to the finite or temporal, but can function freely in the context of infinity and eternity as and when required. Here, there is no struggle for existence—the feral has been transformed into the divine. All existence is mortal. LIFE is immortal. The dichotomy between you, the particular existential being, and the deathless Totality vanishes into the Unitary Wholeness of THE ALONE: *sammā sambuddha*.

A Note on the Text

All the items republished in this collection first appeared in *The Middle Way*, the quarterly journal of the Buddhist Society. Some were specially written; others were transcripts or recensions of talks given under the auspices of the Society, many of them in the early days delivered extempore. The date when each piece was published is given in brackets below its opening titles in the main text.

'That Brāhman, the Buddha' was originally a talk delivered at the Caxton Hall, Westminster, London on 18 November 1953.

'What do we Seek?' was based on a Wesak talk entitled 'The Buddha Taught the Way to Happiness', given in the Caxton Hall on 18 May 1962.

'You Talk, I Listen' was based on a talk given at the Buddhist Summer School on 24 August 1963.

'The Goal' was based on a talk given at the Buddhist Summer School on 22 August 1964.

'Mindfulness and the Fourth Precept' was published with the editorial comment, 'These notes are from a new book which Mr Mehta hopes to complete in due time.' The book referred to must be his *The Heart of Religion* (1976).

The following were all based on talks given at the Buddhist Summer School:

'Wisdom and Compassion' – 30 August 1966;
'The Open and the Hidden' – 24 August 1969;
'Götterdämmerung' – late August (exact date uncertain), 1970;
'The Star and the Bubble' – 21 August 1971;
'Buddhism and Yoga' – 28 August 1972;
'Buddhahood' – late August/early September (exact date uncertain), 1976.

'The Good Friend' was written by request for the special edition of *The Middle Way* celebrating Christmas Humphreys' 80th birthday in 1981.

'The Meaning of Death' was written by request for the special issue of *The Middle Way* on the subject of Death published in 1982.

'The Nature of Meditation' was based on a talk given at the Buddhist Society on 13 October 1971.

The review of Papul Jayakar's book, *Krishnamurti — a Biography* appeared in *The Middle Way* in 1987.

'Living the Good Life', Interviews with Phiroz Mehta by John Snelling, was published in *The Middle Way* in four parts in 1986.

Index